Southern Poets
Edited by Allison Jones

First published in Great Britain in 2007 by:
Young Writers
Remus House
Coltsfoot Drive
Peterborough
PE2 9JX
Telephone: 01733 890066
Website: www.youngwriters.co.uk

All Rights Reserved

© Copyright Contributors 2007

SB ISBN 978 1 84431 281 8

Foreword

Young Writers was established in 1991 and has been passionately devoted to the promotion of reading and writing in children and young adults ever since. The quest continues today. Young Writers remains as committed to the nurturing of poetic and literary talent as ever.

This year's Young Writers competition has proven as vibrant and dynamic as ever and we are delighted to present a showcase of the best poetry from across the UK and in some cases overseas. Each poem has been selected from a wealth of *Little Laureates* entries before ultimately being published in this, our sixteenth primary school poetry series.

Once again, we have been supremely impressed by the overall quality of the entries we have received. The imagination, energy and creativity which has gone into each young writer's entry made choosing the poems a challenging and often difficult but ultimately hugely rewarding task - the general high standard of the work submitted ensured this opportunity to bring their poetry to a larger appreciative audience.

We sincerely hope you are pleased with this final collection and that you will enjoy *Little Laureates Southern Poets* for many years to come.

Contents

Joseph Langridge (11)	1
Kelly Davis (11)	1
Zoe Hughes-Richings (11)	2

Beechwood School, St Peter Port

Harry Brooke (9)	2
Scott Bourgaize (10)	3
Cameron Chalmers (10)	3
Peter Sandwith (11)	4
Thomas Nightingale (8)	5
TJ Fitzgerald (9)	6
Kit Betley (11)	7
Richard Sweeney (11)	8
Jamie Jenner (10)	8
Daniel Lee-Barber (9)	9
Andrew Oxburgh (10)	9
Brendan Ferbrache (10)	10
Daniel Emmerson (9)	10
Hamish Glass (9)	11
Andrew Tautscher (10)	12
Matthew Le Maitre (10)	13
David Brewin (9)	14
Thomas Murphy (9)	15
George Martin (9)	16

Bickleigh Down CE (A) Primary School, Plymouth

Justine Oliver (7)	16
Molly Perryman (11)	17
Jessica Brownhill (9)	18
Emily Hannah Rose (11)	18
Sarah Sheppard (11)	19
Adam Spencer (9)	19
Jessica Morcom (11)	20
Emily Cooper (8)	20
James Garbett (8)	21
Aimee Green (9)	21
Holly Brockendon (9)	22
James Vickery (7)	22
Shaun Temlett (8)	23

Amy Jarvis (9)	23
Hannah Snook (8)	24

Butts Primary School, Alton

Francesca Elizabeth Lawrence (8)	24
Toby Welch (8)	25
Daisy Coates (8)	25
Matthew Heard (8)	25
Joseph Cosgrove (8)	26
Alice Farrington (8)	26
Jayne Milburn (8)	26
Liam Andrew Ham (9)	27
Charlotte Ventham (9)	27
Katie Anderson (9)	27
Eleanor Burden (8)	28
Lloyd Smallwood (9)	28
Zachariah Lenton (9)	29

Chiltern Primary School, Basingstoke

Skyla Penhallurick (11)	29
Callan Wilkinson (10)	30
Hannah Littleboy (11)	31
Christopher Matthews (11)	31
Lauren Flint-Johnson (11)	32
Harley Pitt (11)	32
Charlene Smith (11)	32

Glenfrome Primary School, Eastville

Talia Leigh Barwick (8)	33
Ella Oakley (7)	33
Nadija Jama (8)	34

La Mare de Carteret Primary School, Castel

Liam Chainey (10)	34
Cherise Gaudion (11)	35
Taylor Quate (10)	35
Tom Videlo (11)	36
Kate Sinclair (11)	36
Felix Rice (10)	37
Adam Black (10)	37

Alex Chapman (11)	38
Hamish Erskine (7)	38
Nicole Vaudin (10)	39
Evie Weeks (11)	39
Katrina Reynolds (8)	39
Nicole Guilmoto (10)	40
Joe Le Roux (10)	40

Langrish Primary School, Petersfield

Amelia Scott (10)	40
Natalie Collyer (10)	41
Layla Andrews (10)	41
Harrison Wright (10)	42
Matilda Hall (9)	43
James Henderson (10)	44
Jack Lilleywhite (10)	45
Terri-Anne Dorn (10)	45
Poppy Duncan (10)	46
James Hart (10)	46
Anastasia Pantry (10)	47
Louisa Hammond (10)	47
Sophie Richards (10)	48
Ella Peters (10)	48
Serena Morge (9)	49
Natasha Shelsher (10)	49
Lizzie Grinter (9)	50
Jude Gladstone (10)	51
Jennifer Wheeler (10)	51
Melissa Meredith (10)	52
Emma Carter (10)	52
Amber Smith (10)	53
Georgie Cornish (9)	53
George Cowlrick (9)	54
Ellie Burton (9)	54
Alexander Houghton (9)	54
Teigen Sethi (9)	55
Henry Crosswell (9)	55
Olivia Strick (8)	55
Charlie Cooper (9)	56
Jack Ford (9)	56
Emma Duncan (8)	57

Molly Brown (8)	57
Tom McDermott (8)	58
Dan Egelstaff (9)	58
Ellen Norris (9)	58
Polly Ann Carter (8)	59
Felix Hall (8)	59
William Thomas Matthews (8)	59
Charlie Jane Perrin (8)	60
Emily Hillman (8)	60
Bethany Rose Wickens (8)	61
Connor John Langan (8)	61
Josie Stanesby (8)	62
Katie Hamm (8)	62
Kathleen Robertson (8)	62
Maia Jade Usha Sethi (8)	63
James Bridger (8)	63
Jack Andrew Symes (8)	64
Archie Hill (8)	64

Marhamchurch CE Primary School, Bude

Georgia Ray (11)	65
Jordan Grigg (10)	65
Annie Proudfoot (10)	66
Aimee Grace Mitchell (10)	66
Callum Heywood & Joshua Summers (11)	67
Emma Kitchener (11)	67
Charlotte White (10)	68

Modbury Primary School, Modbury

Catherine Romney (8)	68
Kirsty Lock (9)	69
Tyler Gilley (9)	69
Hannah Brace (9)	70
Liam Twohig (8)	70
Finlay Andrews (9)	71
Jake Harvey-Doddridge (9)	71
Peter Blackler (9)	72
Benjamin Teague (9)	72
Jade Birch (9)	73
Jack Sturton (8)	73
Elliott George (9)	74

Adam Keates (9)	74
Angus West (9)	75
Beth Wilson (9)	75
Billy Jones (9)	76
Jake Beer (9)	76
Jenny Grace (9)	77
Andrew Low (9)	77
Tess Hemsi (9)	78
Mary-Kate Dolley (8)	79
Anna Lee (8)	80
Cecily Edwards (9)	81
Joe Berry (8)	82
Kiera-Louise Snell (8)	83
Beth Holgate (8)	84

Ninfield CE Primary School, Ninfield

Matthew Meade (11)	84
Abbie Nixon (11)	85
Gemma Connor (11)	85
Jules Siviter (11)	86
Zak Barton (11)	86
Rebekka Abel (10)	87
Hallam Earl (10)	87
Vanya Askew (10)	88
Oliver Charles Greene (11)	88
Mohammad Bourner (11)	89
Sophie Roller (10)	89
Ellie Whiting (11)	90
Tommy Hart (11)	91

Ormer House Preparatory School, Alderney

Alicia Bowers (9)	91
Stephanie Dale (11)	92
Joseph Stanley (9)	92

Pensans Community Primary School, Penzance

Lewis Wells (11)	93
Chris McKee Rogers (11)	93
Katie Birchall-Kells (10)	94
Lucy Elizabeth Barker (11)	94
Bethany Blewett (10)	95

Brandon Bugden (11)	95
Jodie Robinson (10)	96
Chris Hocking (10)	96
Sam Skinner (11)	96
Alice Chaplin (11)	97
Cory Austwick (10)	97
Owen Donald Fellows (10)	98
Sophie Weeks (11)	98
Nick Herring (11)	99
Daniel Paul Ferris (10)	99
Hannah Maddern (10)	100

Port Isaac CP School, Port Isaac

Asa Paddock (8)	100
Courtney Summers (8)	100
Harry Hambly (8)	100
Sam Lorimer (7)	101
Liam Murray Strout (8)	101
Tom Penny (8)	101
Sinead Tiddy (8)	101
Gus Houston (9)	102
Holly Hambly (8)	102

Punnets Town CP School, Heathfield

Gaia Hancock (11)	102

Ramsbury Primary School, Ramsbury

Chloe Chidsey (10)	103
Elliot Rai (11)	103
Tara Colsell-Hawes (11)	103
Jamie Goodhew (11)	104
William Ballard (11)	104
Imogene Knight (11)	105
Anya Milner (11)	105
Ellen Little (11)	106
Georgina Perkins (11)	106
Stephanie Milne (11)	106
Maia Pearce (11)	107
George Martin-Johnson (10)	108

St Andrew's Primary School, St Andrew's
Emma Falla (10)	108
Jessica Dean (10)	109
Phoebe Morgan (10)	109
Giles Quigley (9)	109
Freya McLaren (8)	110
Oscar Anderson (10)	110
Beatrice Morgan (8)	111

St Joseph's RC Primary School, Aldershot
Eleanor Greenwood (11)	112
Emily Jones (11)	113
Matthew Hutchinson (11)	114
Sadie Taylor (11)	115
Mollie Spindler (10)	116
Georgia Carpenter (11)	116
Hamish Radford Ross (10)	117

St Martin's Primary School, St Martin's
Pierre Le Poidevin (11)	117
Joanna Richardson (10)	118
Stephanie Bisson (11)	119
Tomos A Geraint Ap Siôn (11)	120
Sarah Keirle (10)	121
George Mason (11)	122
Georgina Prow (11)	123
James Rabey (11)	124
Thomas McConnell (11)	125
Stephanie Johns (11)	126
Alex Domaille (10)	127
Troy Le Page (10)	128

St Mary's CE Primary School, Penzance
Joe Weaver (9)	129
Keziah Sutherns (9)	130
Kieran Lunn (9)	131
Katie Lawrence (9)	132
Paige Maguire (9)	133
Elijah Callon (10)	134

St Neot Community Primary School, Cornwall
Chris Barrett (10)	135
Scott Worthing (11)	135
Daniel Gerry (11)	136
Jacca Cock (11)	136
Barney Wood (9)	137
Tia Wilton (10)	137
Ross Bellringer (10)	138
Ben Symons (11)	138
Kelsie Worth (10)	139
Rhiannon Sanders (11)	139
Adam Gregory (11)	140
Amber Johnson (9)	141
Asha Wilton (11)	142
Liam Parnell (11)	142
Ben Froggatt (10)	143
Ashley Nicholls (11)	143
Rowen Cunningham (11)	144

Sandford School, Sandford
Tania Douglas (9)	144
Lucy Douglas (9)	145

Shirley Junior School, Shirley
Thomas Edwards (8)	145
Molly Oldridge (8)	146
Olivia Beatson (8)	147
Nicolas Neves (8)	148
Albany Rowan (8)	148
Imogen Lee (8)	149
Emily Yeates (7)	149
Tom Harman (8)	150
Toby Wilkins (8)	150
Lydia Keeffe (8)	151
Anna Pugh (8)	151
Joanna Loizou (8)	152
Rosy-May Schofield	152
Matthew Loizou (8)	153
Elizabeth Laybourne (8)	153
Katie Rose Sherliker (8)	154
Grace Masih (7)	154

Alice Wheatley (8)	155
Chloe McArthur (8)	155
Reuben Benton (7)	156
Louis Machin (8)	156
Phoebe Haste (7)	157
Lauren Mara Rickard Foxley (7)	157
Charlotte Franklin (8)	158
James Matthew Quinn (8)	158
Anna Hotston (8)	159

The Tynings CP School, Staple Hill

Nicholas Walker (9)	159
Ocean Bracey (10)	160
Sasha Morch-Monsted (10)	160
Vicky Vallis (10)	161
Matthew Blanchard (9)	161
Kyra Hopkins (10)	162
Joseph Wood (10)	162
Naomi Hall (10)	163
Joshua Hughes (9)	163
Laura Flett (9)	164
Mitchell Brosnan (10)	164
Dominic Porteous (10)	165
Jack Mitchell (10)	165
Hayden Watkins (10)	166
Elliot Lattuca (9)	166
Abbie White (10)	167
Brendan Turner (10)	167
Jacob West (9)	168
Harry Edwards (10)	168
Chris Lewis (10)	169
Abigail Bowden (9)	170
Daniel Sheppard (10)	170
William Stabb (10)	171

Trewirgie Junior School, Redruth

Rebecca Waters (11)	171
Ellie Coleman	172
Jasmin Hoole-Jackson (8)	172
Bailey Watling (8)	172
Isabelle Vincent (8)	173

Gemma George (9)	173
Bethany Zammit (11)	173
Caitlin Roach (8)	174
Kelly Russell (9)	174
Katie McVey (10)	175
Jesse Roach (10)	175
Chloe Dunstan (8)	176
Emily Mae Exelby (8)	176
Emily Youlton (9)	177
Claudia Dominguez (10)	177
Kensa Jose (8)	178
Bethany Ann Moyle (11)	178
Daniel Matthews (8)	179
Kayleigh Richards (10)	179
Naomi Rogers (10)	180
Shannon Massey (9)	181
Bethany Rutter (8)	181
Harry Littlejohns (8)	182
Jacob Woodbridge (8)	182
Saffron Blake (7)	183
Molly Buckland (8)	183
Ashley Sweet (8)	184
Fynley Caudery (8)	184

Windlesham House School, Washington

Connor Wrigley	184
Benjamin Grant	185
James Line (11)	185
Imogen Rough (11)	186
William Dawe (11)	186
Katharine Stocker	187
Sam Fiddian-Green	187
Oliver Micklewright (11)	188
Harry Goodwin (12)	188
Fergus Simpson	189
Georgina Boden	189
Chris Dawe	190
Charlie Perry (11)	190
Miranda Holliday	191
Alastair Maude	191
Claudia Thornett	192

Grace Lee	192
Lily Hinton	193
Daniel Poulton (11)	193
Adam Miller	194
Millie Sparkes	194
Zi Yuan Qu	195
Charlie Fenn	195

The Poems

All About My School

School is for hard work,
School's for learning,
School's for making friends,
I think school's for many things.

The best thing about school
Is when you know it's your football day
And you can't wait to get out and play.

To many people school can be many things
But to me I think school is a big community
Working together.

There's one thing I can tell you about school,
If I didn't go to school,
I wouldn't have half the friends I do have,
So don't just think of it for a place to learn,
Think of it for a place to be friends.

Joseph Langridge (11)

Tesco Jungle

Petrified
Shaking as I try to get through.
Barge or ask, which shall I do?
Trolley slides back,
Knocking me flying.
Grab your children before it happens to them.
Breath catching,
As I get through.
People slithering as they go through the shop.
I race to get out . . .
Reaching for the door
And . . .
Yes, at last.

Kelly Davis (11)

Playground Youngsters' Playgroup

Determinedly wild
As they head for the sand
Grabbing your child as they head for their treat
As they eat their bowl full of sweets
They sing their songs
As the adults grab their tongs
The pipe leaks
Drip, drip, drip
Then I slip
Crash, bang . . .
To be continued . . .

Zoe Hughes-Richings (11)

Orderman

I am Orderman

I know why creatures grow to be big.
I know how many digits in infinity.
I know what happened when the dinosaurs died out.
I know when all of you will die.
I know where witches hide.
I know how to get to the stars.
I know who welcomes you in Heaven.
I know what aliens look like.

I have been a radio forced to play to an empty room.
I have been an ant injured by an unfamiliar foot.
I have been a brick thrown around in the mist.
I have been a ghost that has drifted into secret rooms.
I have been lost in misty marches.
I have been squashed into the side of a small pencil sharpener.
I have been imprisoned in a dark scary castle.
I have been in Santa's workshop when no one's there.

I have been solid and liquid.

I am Orderman.

Harry Brooke (9)
Beechwood School, St Peter Port

Superio

I am Superio

I know why the grass is green and why it covers the world.
I know why sea monsters live on Earth and why.
I know why life is just torture and torment.
I know why death happens.
I know why World War II began and why.
I know God Almighty and where He lives.
I know how life is lived after death.
I know Jesus and how He died.
I have been a turtle in a sea of emotion.
I have been a sewing needle in the cloth of eternity.
I have been an eagle in the morning sun.
I have been a spade in the earth of holy lands.
I have been to Heaven, the golden world.
I have been to other planets never before seen.
I have been to the past shrouded in mystery.
I am the light of dark and the dark of light.

I am Superio.

Scott Bourgaize (10)
Beechwood School, St Peter Port

Mirror Image World

My eyes open,
The world is as dark as death.
I clutch my weapons,
The world is at war.
I crave food,
I search dumps and bins,
Nothing!
My skin is crawling,
How long can I go on in this living hell?
Each raindrop feels like a pin hitting my skin,
I shut my eyes.

Cameron Chalmers (10)
Beechwood School, St Peter Port

Monsters In The Dark

It was late, late at night
By the time I woke up.
My throat was quite dry
So I reached for my cup.

This room is too hot,
I suddenly thought.
I walked to the window
But the latch had been caught.

I'll go find another,
I proceeded to think.
I opened the door
With a soft gentle clink.

I made for the bathroom,
The light, it was on!
Was there something in there?
Was it already gone?

With my hand on the doorknob,
I peeked carefully in.
My knees, they were knocking,
Oh my, what a din!

A huge monstrous shadow
Appeared on the wall.
And I was so frightened,
'Cause I am so small.

Then I started to shake,
Yes I jiggled about.
Would I live to see dawn?
My heart filled with doubt!

The shadow moved closer,
My mouth felt quite dry.
I shut tight my eyelids
And tried not to cry.

My legs would not move
But I wanted to run.
Then I heard the best voice
In the world say, 'Hi Son.'

Peter Sandwith (11)
Beechwood School, St Peter Port

Evening Comes

Evening comes
      with school bell ringing.
Evening comes
      with bath water rushing.
Evening comes
      with teachers marking.
Evening comes
      with pans clashing.
Evening comes
      with sunset coming.
Evening comes
      with bedtime reading.
Evening comes
      with glasses clinking.
Evening comes
      with owls hooting,
      with me sleeping
      and parents cheering.

Thomas Nightingale (8)
Beechwood School, St Peter Port

Evening Comes

Evening comes
      with children walking.
Evening comes
      with people cycling.
Evening comes
      with sunsets setting.
Evening comes
      with owls hooting.
Evening comes
      with church bells ringing.
Evening comes
      with choirs singing.
Evening comes
      with donkeys trotting.
Evening comes
      with lights switching.
Evening comes
      with cars beeping.
Evening comes
      with the moon shining.
Evening comes
      with the boys reading.
Evening comes
      with stars twinkling.
Evening comes
      with animals resting.
Evening comes
      with planes flying.
Evening comes,
      to drag me into bed.

TJ Fitzgerald (9)
Beechwood School, St Peter Port

Ghost

Man scarer
Sword bearer

Cloak wearer
Grim Reaper

Heart ripper
Blood sipper

Undertaker
Body stealer

Stair glider
Head carrier

Faceless monster
Animal slaughterer

Cold finger
Brain drinker

Spineless creature
Horror maker

Dream breaker
Sleep awakener

Life taker
Soul destroyer

The ghost.

Kit Betley (11)
Beechwood School, St Peter Port

Golden Ring

I was strolling along on a hot summer's day,
It might be April, it could be May,
When I came across the strangest thing,
Guess what? An enchanted golden ring!

It's getting dark, I must not linger,
I placed it on my middle finger,
Suddenly a floating genie appeared,
With grey hair and a ginger beard.

Suddenly I had a peculiar feeling,
All my scratches and wounds were healing,
My heart turned black and shades of blue,
My head was a mess, what should I do?

I pulled it off in despair
And hurled it into the misty air.

Richard Sweeney (11)
Beechwood School, St Peter Port

Snakes

Poisonous screaming snakes,
Poison seeping into the body,
Pouncing bloodthirsty eater,
Protecting babies from bears.

Sneaking quietly through the undergrowth,
Slithering jumper biting the victim,
Snapping destroyers,
Screeching striker,
Striking sky.

Biting monstrous creatures,
Hitting directly in the eye,
Creeping silently ready to pounce,
Sucking life out of its victim,
Air-taking monster.

Jamie Jenner (10)
Beechwood School, St Peter Port

If My Cat Left My House . . .
(A poem about my black and white cat called Murphy)

If my cat left my house . . .
He'd miss coming to my room to miaow me goodnight
And then curling himself up in his cosy little bed.
He'd miss his secret hideaway behind the cupboard
And the chance to sleep away the day in peace and quiet.
He'd miss helping Dad to make his big work decisions
And being able to sit on Dad's newspaper - how annoying.
He'd miss running away from a falling leaf
And being frightened by a tiny little bird.
He'd miss being called for his supp-supp-supp
And being given his special dish of Felix fish in jelly.
He'd miss following us around the house like a shadow
And always falling on our feet hoping to be stroked.
He'd miss being reminded of getting stuck under the floor
And when he ran away getting locked in a tool shed for a week,
But most of all he'd miss our kisses and cuddles
And being tickled underneath the chin,
Worst of all we'd miss him too!

Daniel Lee-Barber (9)
Beechwood School, St Peter Port

The Moon

The moon is a piece of cheese
Asking to be eaten.

It's a giant's fingernail
Hanging by a piece of string,
Attached to the giant's castle.

The moon is a shining pendulum
Swinging to and fro.

It's a piece of cake covered in icing,
Begging to be digested.

It's the peak of a mountain
Watching over Planet Earth.

Andrew Oxburgh (10)
Beechwood School, St Peter Port

It Was A Dark And Stormy Night

Wolves howled,
Dogs growled.

The gloomy moon shone
As day was gone.

Dogs were shredded,
Humans beheaded
And guts squished everywhere.

The wind whistled
And humans shouted,
No one running there and about.

Heads here, skulls there
And some skin with someone's hair.

All the streets red with blood,
It was a crisis from above.

Brendan Ferbrache (10)
Beechwood School, St Peter Port

Sloth

Monkey messer,
Canopy grabber,
Cloud reacher,
Snail trailer,
Ugly breeder,
Leaf cruncher,
Slow cruiser,
Bug snapper,
Steady gripper,
Fungi keeper,
Night snorer,
Stink spreader,
Sun waster,
Coconut slurper,
Eternity sleeper.

Daniel Emmerson (9)
Beechwood School, St Peter Port

My Birthday

My birthday comes
With the alarm clock ringing

My birthday comes
And it's so thrilling

My birthday comes
With friends arriving

My birthday comes
With lots of unwrapping

My birthday comes
With tonnes of playing

My birthday comes
With Mummy cheering

My birthday comes
With candles lighting

My birthday comes
With loads of scoffing

My birthday comes
With stomachs aching

My birthday comes
With my friends departing

My birthday comes
With my family singing
Happy birthday to me!

Hamish Glass (9)
Beechwood School, St Peter Port

Lord Excelto

I am Lord Excelto

I know where God and all the angels are.
I know where birds keep plants.
I know how Earth was drawn.
I know how the world will carry on after we're dead.
I know why fish don't have toes.
I know where trees were built.
I have been a lion, the king of the desert.
I have been the sun shining down on Pluto.
I have been an albatross soaring the galaxy.
I have been a dolphin swimming through time and space.
I have been to the middle of the Earth.
I have been a monkey's uncle.
I have been on the red square mountain.
I have been in the misty, secretive yesterday.

I am the sun, I am the moon.

I am Lord Excelto.

Andrew Tautscher (10)
Beechwood School, St Peter Port

The Deadly Beast

It is deathly cold
And black as doom
And all the graves are empty.

Massive footprints cover the ground,
Where the deadly beast has trampled.

Ten heads, eight legs,
Long tongue, short tail.

It leaves tracks where it has destroyed
All obstacles in its path.

Roads turn to rivers of blood,
Nothing moves.

The world goes silent
Except for the screams.

Massive fangs protruding from its jaws,
Ten necks each with its own pair of claws.

The deadly beast is out.

Matthew Le Maitre (10)
Beechwood School, St Peter Port

School Bell Rings

School bell rings
      with children shouting
School bell rings
      with teachers cheering
School bell rings
      with bullies beating
School bell rings
      with teachers marking
School bell rings
      with parents chatting
School bell rings
      with the caretaker cleaning
School bell rings
      with cars all hooting
School bell rings
      with car parks filling
School bell rings so I can rest
      without my teacher moaning!

David Brewin (9)
Beechwood School, St Peter Port

Evening Comes

Evening comes
        with supper cooking,
Evening comes
        with football playing,
Evening comes
        with my brother crying,
Evening comes
        with light dying,
Evening comes
        with parents chatting,
Evening comes
        with teapots clattering,
Evening comes
        with mum's nagging,
Evening comes
        with owls hooting,
Evening comes
        to force me to bed.
Evening's the busiest time of the day.

Thomas Murphy (9)
Beechwood School, St Peter Port

If I Left School I'd Miss . . .

If I left school I'd miss . . .
The guitar cases,
The colourful art displays.

If I left school I'd miss
Miss Le Tissier's piano and singing,
Playground games on sunny days.

If I left school I'd miss . . .
The college cricket ground,
Beanie marching to and fro.

If I left school I'd miss . . .
The fun of the Easter term play,
All our hard work to show.

If I left school I'd miss . . .
My friends and pranks,
Playing tricks when out of sight.

If I left school I'd miss . . .
The rush and tumble,
Tired out, sleeping well at night.

George Martin (9)
Beechwood School, St Peter Port

The Roses Waving In The Wind

In a garden there was a bed of red roses,
It was a windy day.

An old lady had planted them when she was a young girl,
She had watched them grow and their leaves uncurl.
The old lady watched them get more beautiful each day.

In the winter the roses slept,
All through the summer the roses kept the old lady smiling
With their glorious blooms.

Justine Oliver (7)
Bickleigh Down CE (A) Primary School, Plymouth

Petz

I may be sly
With a twinkle in my eye,
My coat is glossy,
But you can trust I won't be bossy.
What am I? A cat!

I burrow deep underground,
I love to leap and bound.
My ears may stick up or down,
You can buy me in any town.
What am I? A rabbit.

I scamper here and there,
I take amazing care.
I squeak when I am happy,
I will never ever be snappy.
What am I? A mouse!

I am bigger than the average pet,
You can use me in a bet.
Some of us are used to a gamble,
Some of us love to ramble.
What am I? A horse!

I flap my wings
And I pack my things.
I soar through the sky
Until the day I die.
What am I? A bird!

I wag my tail all day,
I have a really cool way.
I can do a job on a farm,
Sometimes I hurt my arm.
What am I? A dog!

Man's best friend,
There till the end.
We can be big or small,
But can be enjoyed by all.
What are we? Pets!

Molly Perryman (11)
Bickleigh Down CE (A) Primary School, Plymouth

My Sister

I have a book with 65 pages,
It was on the shelf but now it's gone.
My sister Izzy must have taken it,
I think she did it for a bit of fun.
I looked everywhere,
Even under the stair.
I looked under my bed,
My sister said,
'I think it's in the garden,
I think it's in the sea,
It might be in the garage,
Just hurry with your tea!'
I looked,
I looked,
I looked everywhere.
I even looked behind the stair
And what did I find in my sister's hair?
A ripped page of mine.
Oh, look it's there!

Jessica Brownhill (9)
Bickleigh Down CE (A) Primary School, Plymouth

Fairies

At the bottom of our garden
I think I saw them twice:
They were dancing and playing
And they really looked quite nice.

One evening, when it's quiet,
I'm going to try and see
If I can just creep up on them -
Without them seeing me!

They're lovely-looking fairies
With different coloured wings;
I'd love to try and play with them
And show them all my things.

Emily Hannah Rose (11)
Bickleigh Down CE (A) Primary School, Plymouth

Our World

Frogs and toads
Rats and mice
Fleas and lice
Those are not very nice.

Trees and flowers
Birds, bees
And butterflies
That flutter in the summer breeze.

Day and night
Sun and moon
Rivers and seas
That ebb and flow.

This is our world
Good and bad
It's how God made it
And that makes me glad.

Sarah Sheppard (11)
Bickleigh Down CE (A) Primary School, Plymouth

Basketball

I like to watch basketball,
It is played in a big rectangular hall.
My favourite player is Jamie Burchell,
He is big, hardworking and tall.
My team is the Plymouth Raiders, they play in green,
In every match they are really keen
To win the BBL Trophy.

The players dribble, they shoot, they score,
They rebound, they bounce and more.
Plymouth Raiders work their magic one more time,
Before the buzzer sings its final chime.
Jamie Burchall's the game's MVP,
He signs his autograph just for me.
Afterward he goes home to celebrate.

Adam Spencer (9)
Bickleigh Down CE (A) Primary School, Plymouth

Bickleigh Down

Bickleigh Down, Bickleigh Down is truly the best.
Bickleigh Down, Bickleigh Down is better than the rest.

The teachers are kind and caring and as lovely as can be,
You will have a great time here, and soon you will see

The classes are all great, with some subjects that are cool,
You will fit in right away and begin to love the school.

Lunch and break time are great parts of the day as you can chat
to your friends,
You can also go on great school trips - the fun here never ends!

Great activities for KS1 - show and tell and play
KS2 get to do grown-up things and go back in history for the day.

Mr Jensen and Mr Harding are in charge of music and maths,
Their lessons are always made fun and full of lots of laughs.

Mrs Howson is my Year 6 teacher and she is just truly great,
She hardly ever shouts at you, even if you are late.

So now you know about our school, the one that is the best,
Please remember that Bickleigh Down is definitely above the rest!

Jessica Morcom (11)
Bickleigh Down CE (A) Primary School, Plymouth

Space

Space is ace, I love to study space,
I'll go on a star trek, I'll make friends with a Dalek,
I'll find life on Mars, they'll tell me about the stars,
I'll discover a planet made completely of granite,
I'll orbit the sun, it'll be fun.
Just you see, I'll be home by tea!

Emily Cooper (8)
Bickleigh Down CE (A) Primary School, Plymouth

Alien Friend

I know an alien
That comes from planet Mars,
Her name is rather extraordinary
And she has five space cars.

Her skin is lime-green
And her eyes are a mysterious grey
And she can twist her neck
In a lovely sort of way.

She has alien emotions
And never goes to sleep,
I must say she's very strong,
She could even knock over a jeep.

When she came to me
It was a sunny shiny day,
I was doing Lego
When the alien came to play.

My alien is a good buddy,
She is my best friend,
Now I am really sad
As this poem is about to end.

James Garbett (8)
Bickleigh Down CE (A) Primary School, Plymouth

My Life

My life goes fast,
My life goes slow,
My life is different in every way,
My life is mad,
My life is sad,
But most of all my life is fun.

Aimee Green (9)
Bickleigh Down CE (A) Primary School, Plymouth

I Like The . . .

I like the beach because . . .
The crystal-blue sea shines at me,
The golden sand is as soft as a feather,
The old beach cabin's decorated with heather,
The dolphins are swimming side by side
Even when it's early tide.

I like the park because . . .
The swings go so high
You feel you're touching the sky,
The slides make you go so fast,
The monkey bars climb, climb, climb,
I will be able to in time,
But best of all,
The ice cream stall
Which comes every day
When we play.

I like the zoo because . . .
The animals are so sweet,
Except the lions which eat meat,
The snakes may be scary
But hey the monkeys are hairy,
But most of all
The giraffes are so tall,
(I also love feeding time
When the animals look divine)!

Holly Brockendon (9)
Bickleigh Down CE (A) Primary School, Plymouth

Chocolate

Sticky and sweet,
Liquid with heat.

Yummy and scrummy,
In my tummy.

It's chocolate!

James Vickery (7)
Bickleigh Down CE (A) Primary School, Plymouth

Swimming

When I am swimming
I am grinning
I feel I'm skimming
On top of the water.

When I'm winning
My smile is brimming
From cheek to cheek
I feel like I want to shriek
I am so sleek.

When I receive the award it glimmers in the light
I feel I'm 50 foot in height.
When I return
Home I feel I've had a lot to learn.
Winning isn't everything.

Shaun Temlett (8)
Bickleigh Down CE (A) Primary School, Plymouth

Teachers

Our teacher is Mrs Owen,
So we are in 4 'O'.
Is this a good poem?
I will get better as I grow.
Lots of different teachers
Teach us different things.
Mr Jenson is the maths king,
While Mr Harding sings!
Some teach French, some teach games,
Some do it when it rains.
Now and then they teach in a bunch,
Even when we eat our lunch.

Amy Jarvis (9)
Bickleigh Down CE (A) Primary School, Plymouth

At The Seaside

The day we went down to the seaside
Was the day we had so much fun,
I paddled in the cold wet sea
And played in the warm summer sun.

I dug a big hole and buried
My dad very deep in the sand,
We covered every bit of him
Except for his head and his hands.

I had a very cold lolly,
I went for a donkey ride,
I found a seashell and listened
To the whispering sea inside.

And when it was time to pack up
To say goodbye to the sea,
I wasn't too sad because I had
My shell to take home with me.

Hannah Snook (8)
Bickleigh Down CE (A) Primary School, Plymouth

Love

Love is red like a crimson velvet rose.
Love sounds like hearts beating heavily as one.
It looks like two birds together, fluttering their wings in the wind.
It feels like the sun blazing inside you.
Love smells like freshly squeezed raspberries floating on top of ice cream.
Love tastes of food when you haven't eaten for a week.
It reminds me of friends I haven't seen in ages.

This is love to me!

Francesca Elizabeth Lawrence (8)
Butts Primary School, Alton

Sadness

Sadness is white like a cloudy sky.
Sadness is white like a shining bowl.
Sadness reminds me of an ant dying.
Sadness sounds like a person crying.
Sadness tastes like a rotten apple when you expect a fresh one.
Sadness smells like a yucky flower rotting its petals.
Sadness feels like my heart is killing me with shame.
This is what sadness means to me.

Toby Welch (8)
Butts Primary School, Alton

Happiness

Happiness is purple like a blooming tulip shining in the light.
Happiness looks like a smiling child dancing in the sunlight.
Happiness feels like a warm and cuddly pet.
Happiness smells like a fresh baked loaf of bread.
Happiness tastes like warm chocolate chip cookies.
Happiness sounds like laughing children.
Happiness reminds me of magic.
This is *happiness!*

Daisy Coates (8)
Butts Primary School, Alton

Anger

Anger is black like people hurting our world.
Anger smells like red-hot burning fire.
Anger tastes like red-hot chillies burning in your mouth.
Anger sounds like a roaring lion chasing its prey.
Anger looks like the Devil with his trident.
Anger feels like continuing punches in your chest.
Anger reminds me of clashing arguments.
This is *anger* to me.

Matthew Heard (8)
Butts Primary School, Alton

Fear

Fear is like the dark black sky at night-time.
Fear is like red-hot ashes burning your heart.
Fear sounds like a whimpering dog without a home.
Fear looks like a skeleton alive.
Fear feels like walking on fire.
Fear smells like steam from a red-hot volcano.
Fear reminds me of someone dying from my family.

This is fear to me.

Joseph Cosgrove (8)
Butts Primary School, Alton

Love!

Love is red like beaming, scorching fire.
Love tastes like sweet jam tarts melting slowly in your mouth.
Love feels as safe and as cosy as being with your loving family.
Love sounds like waves splashing calmly up to the velvet sand.
Love looks like diamonds glistening in the fiery sun beaming
out of your heart.
Love smells like fresh juicy strawberries being pressed into juice.
This is love to me!

Alice Farrington (8)
Butts Primary School, Alton

Sadness

Sadness is blue like wet raindrops falling to the ground.
Sadness feels like someone you love working away from home.
Sadness smells like the tang of salty seawater.
Sadness tastes like a warm watery cabbage.
Sadness sounds like a shrieking baby.
Sadness looks like a slippery puddle.
Sadness reminds me of my hamster that died.
This is sadness to me.

Jayne Milburn (8)
Butts Primary School, Alton

Happiness

Happiness is light blue like the sky on a summer's day.
Happiness sounds like a little schoolboy laughing on the field.
Happiness tastes like spaghetti Bolognese waiting on the table.
Happiness smells like a freshly cooked piece of bread.
Happiness looks like a great big grin gliding across my face.
This is what happiness means to me.

Liam Andrew Ham (9)
Butts Primary School, Alton

Fear

Fear is black like the night without stars.
Fear smells like a volcano just about to erupt.
Fear looks like a child in a tipping boat.
Fear feels like a stranger holding a child's hand.
Fear reminds me of peanut butter slithering in my mouth.
Fear sounds like a child tumbling down from an extremely tall tree.

This makes me quake and shiver with fear!

Charlotte Ventham (9)
Butts Primary School, Alton

Anger

Anger is red like an exploding cross face.
Anger looks like a rolling ball of fire tumbling down a hill.
Anger feels like a streak of lightning streaming through your body.
Anger reminds me of a huge house burning down in flames.
Anger sounds like a clap of thunder bellowing in the sky.
Anger tastes like a burnt mushroom slipping down your throat.
This is how anger makes me go all red.

Katie Anderson (9)
Butts Primary School, Alton

Hunger

Hunger is brown like freshly made chocolate
Being delivered to wonderful sweet shops.
Hunger feels like pins in my stomach
Prickling my insides.
Hunger reminds me of starving prisoners,
Crying and calling for food.
Hunger sounds like rasping coughs
From a poor homeless child.
Hunger tastes like rotten strawberries,
When you didn't realise they've gone off.
Hunger smells like vanilla ice cream,
When you've just spent your last penny.

This is what hunger means to me.

Eleanor Burden (8)
Butts Primary School, Alton

Fun

Fun is blue like the deep blue sea.
Fun smells like candyfloss at the fair.
Fun looks like people running around being crazy.
Fun feels like the day will never end.
Fun reminds me of all the people I know.
Fun tastes like my favourite thing for tea.
This is what fun is for me.

Lloyd Smallwood (9)
Butts Primary School, Alton

Hatred

Hatred is as red as boiling lava.
Hatred tastes like bad trouble.
It smells like a rotten prune.
It looks like a scalding volcano.
Hatred feels like a thumping heart.
It sounds like trouble.
This is hatred to me.

Zachariah Lenton (9)
Butts Primary School, Alton

The Train Journey

The train is here,
People rushing
Like a herd of ants,
Very noisy, not just me.

Super cold, huge suitcases,
Shopping bags, all shapes and sizes.

I'm stuck next to a smelly stranger,
I'm hungry, yet no one cares.
Baby screaming in my ear,
Trees zoom past, missed in a blink.

Super cold, huge suitcases,
Shopping bags, all shapes and sizes.

A thousand faces in one carriage,
Posters advertise new drinks.
Slowing down, journey over,
Hotel calls and my bed!

Skyla Penhallurick (11)
Chiltern Primary School, Basingstoke

A Journey

People pushing,
People shoving,
Can't hear talking,
Very annoying!

Pain,
Pain,
Steam train;
So slow,
Won't it go
Fast,
Fast?

Old person
Next to me,
Screaming girl,
Very annoying!

Pain,
Pain,
Steam train;
So slow,
Won't it go
Fast,
Fast?

Callan Wilkinson (10)
Chiltern Primary School, Basingstoke

School

S is for science - lots of stuff to do!
Dissection and explosions,
Experiments too.

C is for chemistry - making chemicals,
Mix solids, liquids, gases,
Making weird colours.

H is for history - looking at the past,
Artifacts and pictures,
Learning lots so fast.

O is for onomatopoeia - making lots of sounds,
Crash, bang, wallop, splish, splash, splosh!
Hitting to the ground.

O is for orienteering - finding where to go,
Use your compass, find your map.
Get ready, set, go!

L is for literacy - different types to do,
Story, letter and report.
Don't you go, boohoo!

Learning lots at school,
Will help you lots in the years,
If you learn this rule!

Hannah Littleboy (11)
Chiltern Primary School, Basingstoke

The Light

Into the shadows, into the night,
Into the darkness with no light;
Out of the tunnel, into the station
Roaring as it goes.

Out of the station, into the streets,
Over the river, munching my sweets;
Into the station, off the train,
Wander through streets, home again.

Christopher Matthews (11)
Chiltern Primary School, Basingstoke

Summer's Beauty

Summer has an eyelid of sky-blue,
A pupil of pure shining gold.
She warms you up in seconds though,
Grab some water, ice-cold.

Summer's beauty is amazing,
So pretty, sweet and radiant.
Every aspect of her is stunning,
How can a season be so elegant?

Lauren Flint-Johnson (11)
Chiltern Primary School, Basingstoke

Snow

Snow falls like sugar on a birthday cake.
Snow flickers down from the dull blue sky.
The world becomes a blanket of ice.
Winter has begun.

Harley Pitt (11)
Chiltern Primary School, Basingstoke

On The Train

Here comes the train, I fight for a seat,
Plenty of people for me to greet.
    People eating,
    People meeting,
    People walking,
    People talking.
    Some in a good mood,
    Some biting on food,
    Standing at the door,
    There's more and more.
People all over the place,
A sea of different faces.

Charlene Smith (11)
Chiltern Primary School, Basingstoke

Ant Poem

An ant can't do many things.
It does not have wings.
They can't fly
But they can say goodbye.
Can they bake?
Do they slither like a snake?
Can they think?
Do they blink?
Do they run?
Do they like a bun?
What do they do?
Where do they go to the loo?

Talia Leigh Barwick (8)
Glenfrome Primary School, Eastville

My Dog Gizmo

Playful, funny,
As cute as a bunny,
Chews my boots
And digs for roots.

My dog Gizmo
Has won a dog show,
By dancing
And balancing,
I love him so.

Ella Oakley (7)
Glenfrome Primary School, Eastville

Young Cat

There was a young cat in the street
And tuna was all she would eat.
She ate it all day
Until her tummy said hey!
And was sick all over her feet.

Nadija Jama (8)
Glenfrome Primary School, Eastville

Bombers' Moon

One night in bed,
Hearing planes above me,
Sirens screeching,
Black night,
Grey sadness,
Red fires,
Dad, Dad
In the shelter quickly,
Safe for now.

Liam Chainey (10)
La Mare de Carteret Primary School, Castel

Ladybird

Ladybird,
Her wings sway like a second-hand clock,
Gently, gently they tick,
Flying away as peacefully as the wind.

Her spots are like black splodges of paint,
Drip, drip, drop,
Hiding in the shadows.

She is so small she will disappear before your eyes,
Going, going gone,
Trying to get away.

Her legs are sticky like octopus legs,
Stick, stick, stick,
Climbing up the wall.

Her feelers are as sensitive as a chick,
Flowing, flowing, flowing,
Touching everywhere she goes.

Cherise Gaudion (11)
La Mare de Carteret Primary School, Castel

Fireworks All Around

The 5th of November
Is a wonderful night,
When bonfires and fireworks
Make the dark sky so bright.

The crackers, sparklers, rockets
Are such a sight to see,
They can be very dangerous
So you must go carefully.

So make sure that all your pets
Are safely locked inside,
As all the noise may frighten them
To run away and hide.

Taylor Quate (10)
La Mare de Carteret Primary School, Castel

The Cheetah Was Made
(Based on 'Cat Began' by Andrew Matthews)

For his brain he took the sharpness of an SAS soldier
The wisdom of an owl
And the intelligence of Einstein

For his fur he took the camouflage of a commando
The sleekness of a super car
And the softness of a sponge

For his speed he stole the raw power of a jet plane
The pounding of a heart
And the acceleration of a rocket

For his bite he took the strength of a digger
The violence of the wind
And the timing of a stopwatch

For his legs he took the strength of a bodybuilder
The synchronisation of an athlete
And the swipe of a credit card

Cheetah was made.

Tom Videlo (11)
La Mare de Carteret Primary School, Castel

The Lonely Beach

The lonely beach was quiet and cold
But suddenly Storm came.
He splashed and kicked in the sea.

The moon shone its natural torch down
To show the lost and sad sailors' spirits
The way home to see their loved ones.

The clouds poured buckets of frighteningly cold water
Down on the golden sand.

Then Storm left
And once again the beach was lonely.

Kate Sinclair (11)
La Mare de Carteret Primary School, Castel

Aye-Aye Began
(Based on 'Cat Began' by Andrew Matthews)

Aye-Aye began,
For his eyes he took the roundness of the moon,
The sight of an eagle, the colour of amber.

For his middle nail he took the length of a barge,
The strength of a bodybuilder,
The skull of Ronaldinho.

For his character he took the shyness of a hedgehog,
The curiosity of a baby,
The awareness of a meerkat.

For his senses he took the hearing of an eagle,
The smell of a dog,
The touch of an angel.

For his fur he took the softness of a feather,
The blackness of coal,
The warmth of a fire
And Aye-Aye was made.

Felix Rice (10)
La Mare de Carteret Primary School, Castel

The Germans Are Coming

Sirens screeching,
The shouting and the weeping,
The Germans are coming,
Run to the shelter,
Bombs booming, exploding,
Crashing down on the ground.
The chugging engines of the planes above,
Then silence.
The families stand there stunned,
Devastated, astonished,
Staring at the remains of what used to be a home.
Everyone joyous and excited that no one got hurt.

Adam Black (10)
La Mare de Carteret Primary School, Castel

How Rabbit Was Made
(Based on 'Cat Began' by Andrew Matthews)

For her hop
She took the bounce of a basketball,
She took the power of the wind.

She stole the brownness of a branch,
She stole the shape of a leaf
To make her ears.

At night
She captured the brightness of the sun,
She captured the twinkle of the stars
To make her eyes.

For her tail
She found the whiteness of a cloud,
She found the softness of a snowball.

For her fur
She copied the movement of the grass,
She copied the colour of a chocolate bar.

She borrowed the whiteness of the snow,
She borrowed the shape of an icicle
To make her teeth.

Rabbit was born!

Alex Chapman (11)
La Mare de Carteret Primary School, Castel

Fear

My fear is grey like a fierce werewolf.
It tastes like radioactive poison.
It smells like toxic green gas.
It looks like a mutant crocodile staring at me.
It sounds like UFOs abducting humans.
It feels like getting crushed by gravity's pull.

Hamish Erskine (7)
La Mare de Carteret Primary School, Castel

Blitz

Bombs falling *boom, bang!*
Footsteps running mad.
People weeping, keeping safe.
Planes dropping, exploding bombs.
Listen for the milkman,
Hear the bottles *clink, clank.*
People scared, getting hurt,
Running through the ruined streets.
Will the shelter protect the children?
Hear the siren again and again.

Nicole Vaudin (10)
La Mare de Carteret Primary School, Castel

The Run

The clouds lined up together ready to start their race.
The trees waved their stiff arms cheering on the runners.
The wind blew his whistle to start the race.
The thunder growled chasing the runners along.
The clouds could see the white seagulls at the end of the sky.
The sun beamed down on the winning cloud as it sprinted across
                                                      the finish line.

Evie Weeks (11)
La Mare de Carteret Primary School, Castel

Happiness

My happiness is green like the grass blowing in the wind.
It tastes like a ripe apple growing on an enormous tree.
It smells like the fire burning through the night.
It looks like fireworks blowing up in the night sky.
It sounds like the beautiful bird tooting in the tall tree.
It feels like the warm wind blowing on me.

Katrina Reynolds (8)
La Mare de Carteret Primary School, Castel

Fireworks Poem

F iring into the sky
I gniting into a bright streak of light
R ising
E xploding
W hooshing
O ff into the inky blackness
R ocketing around space
K aboom!
S parkling into thousands of stars.

Nicole Guilmoto (10)
La Mare de Carteret Primary School, Castel

Bombed

I'm home alone.
The siren has started to screech,
I run to the shelter.
Now I feel black and distressed,
I'm trying to think about Mum.
I come out of the shelter . . . my house is destroyed.
I'm walking to town, a man is telling me my mum is dead.
I'm looking around, there is destruction everywhere,
I'm scared, I'm alone.

Joe Le Roux (10)
La Mare de Carteret Primary School, Castel

Pollution

Pollution, pollution is such a disgrace
Litter on the ground doesn't make it a place
Petrol in cars making it smell
Factories belching out smoke
Making it not very pleasant.

Amelia Scott (10)
Langrish Primary School, Petersfield

Conservation

Pollution is bad, it doesn't make people glad,
From the litter on the floor to the smoke next door,
The car fumes in the air where the world feet unfair,
Why do we do this?

The water that is wasted from our taps,
Could be going to our water butt to save water,
Why are we doing this?

Deforestation is bad, it doesn't make people glad,
From animals with no food to people with no homes,
Why do we cut down trees? We need them for oxygen,
Why do we do this?

Animals disappearing is bad, it doesn't make people glad,
From poachers killing for skin
And hunters destroying the habitat,
We *can* stop this!

Natalie Collyer (10)
Langrish Primary School, Petersfield

Our World

Our world is being turned into a giant disaster,
As the cars and lorries race faster and faster,
Filling our lungs with clouds of smoke,
They don't care at all that they're choking us folk.

Forests and woods are being chopped down,
This makes the poor, innocent animals frown,
They have no say in this serious matter
And haven't enough food on the platter.

There is a way we can save the world if we really try,
We can work it out so no creature or person will die,
You can help the world by using energy-saving lights
And not to forget to turn your TV off at night.

Layla Andrews (10)
Langrish Primary School, Petersfield

Palm Oil

Trees chopped down
Rainforests disappearing
How do we save them?
Don't buy too much palm oil.

Orang-utans on fire
Sloths with no home
How do we save them?
Don't buy too much palm oil.

Palm oil's as popular as Mauritius
We can make it as unpopular as thunder.

Paying people with no money
To make them help to chop down trees
How do we save them?
Don't buy too much palm oil.

We can't blame the workers who chop down trees
Earning money for their families
How do we save them?
Don't buy too much palm oil.

Palm oil's as popular as Mauritius
We can make it as unpopular as thunder.

Sloths and orang-utans
Workers and trees
How do we save them?
Don't buy too much palm oil.

Harrison Wright (10)
Langrish Primary School, Petersfield

Deforestation

Our names are
Borris, Morris and Horris.

We have lived a life
With a big shiny knife.

We look around and what do we see?
Wonderful plant life and lots of trees.

The animals look sad but we cut all the trees down
Wearing a big serious frown.

We really don't mean to pollute,
All of their luscious tropical fruit.

Everyone wants to know do we care.
We tell them no and everyone would stare.

We waste a lot of trees by throwing paper away,
Not using the recycling system people say.

We were wandering around out of a job
When we met a good bloke whose name was Bob.

He gave us this brilliant job,
This fabulous chap Bob.

This job is a diddle, a doddle, a do
And a brilliant chance to raise money for you.

We really want you (about deforestation) to think what you think
But to tell the truth we have a very little link.

Deforestation is not good for animals,
We can solve this problem.

Matilda Hall (9)
Langrish Primary School, Petersfield

Conservation

If you fly to Spain
On a plane,
Don't forget you're polluting the Earth,
All the fumes kill animals
And choke, choke, choke,
So plant some trees and don't fly to Spain
On a plane,
If you do animals die.

If you go to Scotland you kill
The animals on the choking fumes,
Kill, kill, kill.

If you cut down trees
You kill animals I think,
Thirty-five a day is enough to become extinct,
Some cutting down trees,
So don't, don't, don't,
Cut down trees.

We lose a person in Africa every thirty seconds,
I think that's enough
Because if we pollute
The people in Africa
Will be extinct,
So stop polluting and pick up litter,
Don't fly to Spain
On a plane,
If you do plant
Some trees and make more leaves
To save the animals
So we can have a
Beautiful world.

James Henderson (10)
Langrish Primary School, Petersfield

Conservation

Why do people cut down trees?
Why do people kill rare fish in seas?

Why? Because we wasted our lives.
Why? Because we don't think about the animal that dies.

Why is there rubbish? Is seems unfair.
Why does rubbish litter the air?

Why? Rubbish is meant for bins
Not for littering other things.

Why are animals hungry?
Why are they angry?

Why? Because we take their food.
Why? Because we take tigers' claws, it puts them in a bad mood.

Why should we hurt them?
Why don't we recycle or give it to a secondhand shop?

Why? Because it's too much hassle so we just stop. Why?
Animals help us, so we should help them,
Don't throw away paper, plastic or tins,
Put recycled things in some recycle bins!
Dry elephants' tears and open eagles' wings!

Jack Lilleywhite (10)
Langrish Primary School, Petersfield

Recycle

R ecycling is a possibility.
E veryone can join in our environment.
C an you help recycle?
Y ou need to recycle cans and tins.
C an we afford to keep throwing things away?
L et's all work together for the environment.
E arth needs saving.

Terri-Anne Dorn (10)
Langrish Primary School, Petersfield

Animal Life

Trees are falling down and down,
To make way for a brand new town!
It's making all the animals sad,
Because their habitat's gone from good to bad!

The forest is disappearing at an alarming rate
And all the animals must face their fate!
The creatures can't find enough food,
This puts them into starving mood!

The baby cubs are turning ill,
Because there isn't enough food to fill!
So help us to fulfil our task,
We need it done extremely fast!

If we win this mighty fight,
The animals will have food to bite!
So come and help or you'll fret
And your punishment will be regret!

Poppy Duncan (10)
Langrish Primary School, Petersfield

Water

The water in the ocean wide
Is getting dirtier every tide
Because of all the oil spills
The thin black liquid hurts and kills

People turning the taps off
Means that water; we'll have enough
People using water butts
Saving water for their huts

If everyone remembers to recycle water
There will be plenty left for our sons and daughters
Polluting the rivers means the animals die
So help them now so give it a try.

James Hart (10)
Langrish Primary School, Petersfield

The African Elephant

They sway their trunks from side to side,
And flap their giant ears.
Why do people take their tusks
And ignore the elephant's tears?

The ground may shake, they stamp and stomp,
Running away from you,
Yes, you, the hunters, stay away,
It's a horrendous thing to do.

What have they done to make you kill?
Would you pull them apart?
Don't hurt them, they just want to live.
So please don't shoot them with a dart.

Models, statues and piles of ivory,
Don't turn them into these things.
So let elephants live through summers,
Winters, autumns and springs.

Anastasia Pantry (10)
Langrish Primary School, Petersfield

Pollution

Smoke coming out of chimneys,
Grey smoke everywhere,
Petrol is dripping,
Car fumes in the air.

Litter on the ground,
Litter here and there,
Why don't you throw it in the bin?
People just don't care.

Factories making it worse,
Factories producing smoke,
You're not helping the world,
Don't you realise you're making people choke.

Louisa Hammond (10)
Langrish Primary School, Petersfield

Pollution

The blackening darkness in the sky,
All the children asking why?
What do we do?
Stop selling cars
Or do we all shoot off to Mars?

Sweet toffee wrappers on the floor,
Everyone keeps on asking for more,
What do we do?
Stop making sweets
Or do we just keep eating treats?

The blazing sun gets hotter and hotter,
The ice caps disappear till they're just a blur,
What do we do?
Stop making petrol
Or do we just stop life altogether?

Sophie Richards (10)
Langrish Primary School, Petersfield

Pollution

Don't go and buy some motor cars,
You're putting animals behind bars,
If you travel by an aeroplane,
You should feel some shame.

Look at all the factories,
Why don't you recycle batteries?
And don't be a quitter,
Just look at the fumes,
The flowers won't bloom,
Things are so bad,
You are driving the animals mad.

Ella Peters (10)
Langrish Primary School, Petersfield

My Cat Rocky

I have a cat
The same colour as a bat
He likes to catch mice
He thinks they taste nice
In the morning
Without any warning
He bites my dad's feet
He thinks they are meat

In the garden he plays
In lots of different ways
He chases the bees
And whacks into trees
He miaows for his food
Be quick, or he gets in a mood
He sleeps at night on my bed
Sometimes he ends up on my head!

Serena Morge (9)
Langrish Primary School, Petersfield

Pollution

Endangered animals are getting extinct.
Some of them are linked to bread,
But some of them are dead.
Hunters keep on killing the animals for food
And are cutting down the animals' homes,
But such lovely animals are in the forest.
Instead of animals getting extinct,
I think they should go to the zoo to be looked after.
Such a misery for these animals.
Why?
Why do they have to be killed and be eaten?
Why?
I feel sorry for these animals because they keep dying.

Natasha Shelsher (10)
Langrish Primary School, Petersfield

Will The Animals Survive?

Will the animals survive?
Will they live?
Will we find a solution
To stop this pollution?
Will they live a life
Without, through their leg, a knife?
Will we tragically pollute
All their luscious tropic fruit?
Will the animals survive?
Will they live?

Will the animals survive?
Will they live?
Will the animals become rare?
The animals, do we scare?
The trees to them, we rip and tear,
But, what do we care?
Will the animals survive?
Will they live?

Will the animals survive?
Will they live?
The animals find empty cans of Coke,
Then there are factories making smoke,
Some animals will be a pet,
A new family will be met
Or for a zoo, caged
And in there, they will be outraged!
Will the animals survive?
Will they live?

Will the animals survive?
Will they live?
To the animals, land we should give,
So the animals can properly live.
Will we go to the jungle main?

Will we cut down the trees with a crane?
Will the animals face pain
In our unconserved jungle rain?
The floor is vibrating, there is a rumble
And down will come our precious jungle!

Lizzie Grinter (9)
Langrish Primary School, Petersfield

The Writer's Point Of View

Trees fall down . . . *timber!*
The animals lose their homes
But we sit back and relax and watch TV
Which we leave on standby.
Why waste this world?

The animals, moving tree to tree, finding a place to live
But soon to move again,
They think that God has cursed them,
Thinking there's no good in the world.
The latest PM orders to cut down more trees.

Jude Gladstone (10)
Langrish Primary School, Petersfield

Life All Around The World

The world is going round and round
So make sure the pollution can't be found.
The dirt is making us go away
So make a reason so it can go today.

The animals are racing,
Hunger is their fate,
All the people are making their lives so faint.

The rainforest is full of litter and broken trees,
It makes my heart like broken leaves.

Jennifer Wheeler (10)
Langrish Primary School, Petersfield

Conservation

Food disappearing!
Hunters appearing!

Factories and litter,
What can happen next?

Pollution!
Delusion!

Petrol and car fumes,
What can happen next?

Water!
Slaughter!

Smoke and oil spills,
What can happen next?

Sea!
Animals flee!

Pollution,
What can happen next?

Melissa Meredith (10)
Langrish Primary School, Petersfield

Rainforests And Jungles

The rainforests are becoming small and bare,
While the animals are hungry, homeless, no one cares.

Not many monkeys, frogs or trees,
Not many dolphins left in the seas.

Not many insects left at all,
Except for some which are tiny and small.

The flowers are disappearing faster and faster,
While we are creating lots of disasters.

Only a few creatures left in the world,
They are all falling away in one big swirl.

Emma Carter (10)
Langrish Primary School, Petersfield

Water

Water we care for
Water we use
Water the world more

Turn off the taps when you clean your teeth
Save the water, save the water
To help a tree grow another leaf

The water butts leaking
The water butts leaking
Water wasted
While you're sleeping

Don't flush away extra water
That's water we could use
Water, water, water, water
It can kill but it can save you.

Amber Smith (10)
Langrish Primary School, Petersfield

Bees

Here come the bees,
Buzzing,
Searching for some pollen
To turn into honey.

Swarming together,
Working like an army
They do their job.

But . . .
If you get too close
They could sting
And the bee would die.

So . . .
Let the bees do their *job!*

Georgie Cornish (9)
Langrish Primary School, Petersfield

Planet Poem

The stars at night
Glisten in the moonlight.
A star in flight
Makes a wonderful sight,
Twinkles and shimmers
Like rapids on a river.
In the night sky
Look by and by,
You might see a bear
Hiding in its lair.

George Cowlrick (9)
Langrish Primary School, Petersfield

Conservation!

The water that goes down the drain,
Is a massive amount.
The hunters or poachers that kill the animals,
Do they realise? I doubt.
The litter on the ground is getting even worse,
But this is conservation, it's a curse.

Ellie Burton (9)
Langrish Primary School, Petersfield

Pollution

P is for pollution
O is for oil spill
L is for litter
L is for litter everywhere
U is for underestimated smoke
T is for train fumes
I is for I think smoke is bad
O is for oxygen
N is for natural petrol.

Alexander Houghton (9)
Langrish Primary School, Petersfield

The Cosmic Dragon

In the centre of the galaxy
A great cosmic dragon soars
Trapping unsuspecting planets in its mighty jaws
To any nearby systems it is the blackest of foes
By devouring all their energy
The dragon slowly grows
When there are no more left to eat
You can hear the dragon snore
Until a nebular burst forth stars
Then the dragon *roars* once more.

Teigen Sethi (9)
Langrish Primary School, Petersfield

The Best Dragon Ever

The best dragon has a tail as long as a house,
Claws as big as the tallest human on Earth,
Slimy big scales upon his back as big as tiles,
He is as big as two skyscrapers put together, wow!
His fire can go faster than sound and round Earth,
His wings are as wide as five thousand eagles,
Millions of jewels guarded by his huge, thick, scaly hands,
Now that is the best dragon ever, he's *ace!*

Henry Crosswell (9)
Langrish Primary School, Petersfield

Seasons

S pring flowers burst in to life and lambs are born,
E ach day the weather changes from cold to warm,
A mazing brilliant summer in the warm sun,
S ummer season is fun for everyone,
O n autumn days the leaves crunch scattered all around,
N ow it is winter the snow is on the ground,
S *easons change!*

Olivia Strick (8)
Langrish Primary School, Petersfield

My Solar System

Upon my bedroom ceiling my solar system sits,
It's made of plastic balls and wires and several other bits.
It sits there motionless all day
But when it's dark it is time to play.
I press the switch to light the sun
And hear the motor start to run.
The planets start to slowly spin,
I quickly put my CD in.
I lie back down and turn my face
Up to see my very own 'space'.
The lady's voice begins to talk,
Each planet moves on its wire stalk.
The planets all orbit the sun,
Each one separately one by one.
The yellow sun in the centre sits,
Mercury's sphere is nearest it.
Then comes Venus, and next the Earth,
Followed by Mars with its red surface.
Jupiter's next, the lady's voice sings,
Then yellowy Saturn and all its rings.
Uranus is next - we can just see
Neptune - blue-green just like our sea.
Furthest away Pluto rests in space deep,
Silently, I have fallen asleep.
My solar system is switched off at night,
Replaced by the moon and its soft white light.

Charlie Cooper (9)
Langrish Primary School, Petersfield

Space

Space is huge,
Space is vast,
Space holds the secrets of the past.
The stars and planets twizzle and turn,
All the sun does is twizzle and burn.

Jack Ford (9)
Langrish Primary School, Petersfield

Planets

Jupiter is the biggest planet,
So I was told by cousin Janet.

Saturn with her golden rings,
Makes one ask about wondrous things.

Uranus is a sweet sea-blue,
It would be great to visit, just me and you.

Neptune with his turquoise colour,
He is not at all less duller.

The Earth is nearly green all over,
Except for the sea and the white cliffs of Dover.

Venus is golden yellow,
You could never feel any more mellow.

Mercury's one of the closest planets to the sun,
It would be hot but very fun.

Mars is the brightest red star in Earth's sky,
Lots of people wonder why.

Pluto is a dwarf planet,
I also heard this from cousin Janet.

They all rotate around the sun,
Which spreads its warmth to everyone.

Emma Duncan (8)
Langrish Primary School, Petersfield

Stargazing

I see stars glistening in the moonlight
And it is a beautiful clear night.
The stars appear to be so bright,
I look up at the full moon and it gives off so much light.
I am stargazing at midnight,
When I should be asleep with my eyes shut tight.

Molly Brown (8)
Langrish Primary School, Petersfield

Daffodils

Daffodils are so pretty,
Daffodils are so firm,
Daffodils are so yellow,
Daffodils face to the sun.

Daffodils glow in the sun,
Daffodils glint at you,
There are many types of them,
Daffodils are so bright.

Daffodils come when snowdrops die,
Daffodils are so beautiful,
Daffodils make snowdrops look tiny,
Daffodils! Daffodils! Daffodils!

Tom McDermott (8)
Langrish Primary School, Petersfield

Outside

Outside is a warm sunny delight,
A place not to have a fight.
Hear the twittering birds,
Up there in flocks, seagulls near the docks.
Butterflies, insects, bugs so small,
Trees, churches, houses tall.

Dan Egelstaff (9)
Langrish Primary School, Petersfield

Space

S un is the mother of space,
P luto knows his rightful place,
A stronauts go to and fro
C omets whizz fast and slow,
E xtraordinary *space!*

Ellen Norris (9)
Langrish Primary School, Petersfield

Conservation

C are for the environment
O rang-utans are in danger
N ew nature
S tand up for wildlife
E nvironment
R ecycling
V iruses are spreading
A nimals are harmless
T ry to stop
I will recycle cans and newspaper
O rang-utans are in danger
N ew species of animals.

Polly Ann Carter (8)
Langrish Primary School, Petersfield

Conservation

Save our wildlife,
It would make it a quiet life,
Zebras, lions and one cheeky monkey,
(Who is very funky),
Pick up litter from the ground,
Which has been found,
Stop! Global warming,
It is there giving us a warning!

Felix Hall (8)
Langrish Primary School, Petersfield

Conservation

Conservation means protect animals,
Conservation means saving lives,
Conservation means live,
I'm going to do conservation.

William Thomas Matthews (8)
Langrish Primary School, Petersfield

Conservation

C lean up your litter,
O rang-utans are being made extinct,
N ever drop rubbish,
S top global warming,
E nergy is running out,
R ecycle your rubbish,
V ets need more staff,
A nimals are becoming extinct,
T rees give us oxygen,
I nsects are being killed,
O xygen is in us,
N o killing creatures.

Conservation!

Charlie Jane Perrin (8)
Langrish Primary School, Petersfield

Conservation

C reatures are in danger
O striches are killed for their feathers
N ever kill
S ome animals are furry
E lephants have long trunks
R ecycle as much as you can
V ets need more help
A nimals are harmless
T ennis will keep you fit
I nsects are being killed
O ctopuses are being killed
N ature is special.

Emily Hillman (8)
Langrish Primary School, Petersfield

Conservation

C reatures are getting killed.
O xygen is precious.
N ature.
S top global warming.
E nvironment is special and needs more care.
R ecycle more.
V ets need more help.
A nimals are nice.
T rees give us oxygen.
I nsects need help.
O rang-utans are endangered.
N ever destroy nature.

Conservation is cooooool!

Bethany Rose Wickens (8)
Langrish Primary School, Petersfield

Conservation

C onkers off conker trees
O rang-utans need our help
N ature and all the things in the world
S ave the trees and the animals
E arth makes the Earth a better place
R ubbish, don't forget to pick up your rubbish
V egetables, eat more vegetables to keep healthy
A nd look after the animals
T urtles are becoming extinct
I cebergs are melting, polar bears need help fast
O cean has lots of wildlife
N est is warm for the baby chicks.

Connor John Langan (8)
Langrish Primary School, Petersfield

Conservation

The animals are leaping,
The song birds are tweeting,
The field mice are squeaking
And the parrots are screeching.

The spiders are spinning,
The treetops are waving,
The fish are swimming
And the rabbits are hopping.

Josie Stanesby (8)
Langrish Primary School, Petersfield

Animals

A nimals are funny.
N ever kill animals.
I slands have animals on.
M onsters are not real.
A nimals are harmless.
L ions are very funny.
S ome animals are not hairy.

I love animals!

Katie Hamm (8)
Langrish Primary School, Petersfield

Animals

A nimals are living,
N ame one if you can,
I myself would choose a cat
M ight you choose a bat?
A re we looking after them?
L ive a life with animals.

Kathleen Robertson (8)
Langrish Primary School, Petersfield

Conservation

C ars' exhausts are bad for the environment.
O rang-utans are in danger.
N ever kill animals.
S chools in Africa need cleaner water.
E lephants can sometimes be harmless.
R everse killing.
V iruses are spreading.
A nimals are endangered.
T ry not to put litter on the floor.
I gloos are melting.
O ceans are getting rougher.
N ature needs protecting.

Maia Jade Usha Sethi (8)
Langrish Primary School, Petersfield

Conservation

C rocodiles are endangered.
O rang-utans are endangered.
N ever throw litter.
S top this now!
E nvironment - we have to look after.
R ecycling is a must.
V ery low population of tigers.
A nything can die.
T op of the world is a cold place.
I am going to help them.
O pen your heart.
N ever pollute the world again!

James Bridger (8)
Langrish Primary School, Petersfield

Conservation

C reate new nature.
O pen new wildlife centres.
N ew life for young ones.
S tand up for nature.
E ndangered animals should not be in danger.
R everse killing.
V ixens are endangered.
A nimals are harmless to us.
T ry to save wildlife.
I ce is melting.
O rang-utans are endangered.
N o killing!

Jack Andrew Symes (8)
Langrish Primary School, Petersfield

Spiders

Spiders,
I like them
And they like me.
I like them
Because they are dangerous.
I like them
Because they're poisonous.
I like them
Because they're scary
And I like spiders.

Archie Hill (8)
Langrish Primary School, Petersfield

Starer

Stare

There's a little girl in my class who stares
The thing is she stares into thin air
If she sits next to you, you start to stare too
And that's the girl who stares

Chatter

There's a girl in my class who chatters
She thinks it's all that matters
You can get earache as she chats, chats away
And that's the girl who chatters

Fiddle

There's a girl in my class who fiddles
It gets annoying after a little
As she curls her brown hair and puts her elbows everywhere
And that's the girl who fiddles.

Georgia Ray (11)
Marhamchurch CE Primary School, Bude

Beach

On the beach I am sitting
The lullaby of the ocean soothes me to sleep
But the screech of the seagulls awaken me
The pebbles are dancing with my feet
As I leave the calm scene behind me.

I'm here again on this hot sunny day
The sun's smiling down at me
The seaweed sways as it dances the waltz
Then the sand sinks my feet as I leave.

Jordan Grigg (10)
Marhamchurch CE Primary School, Bude

Pussycat

I am a pussycat sitting by the fire
I am ginger, a tomcat many people admire
My eyes are blue and sparkle at night
Many little mice I have given a fright
I laze around, sleeping all day,
Waiting for my owners to come home and play . . .
My name is Arthur, I am 2 years old
Often I worry that I will be sold
I have a furry sister
Who is black and white
We very often have a furious fight
She thinks she is supreme
She thinks that she is better than the Queen
I hope that she will be sold and I will be free
Happy endings, *tee hee hee!*

Annie Proudfoot (10)
Marhamchurch CE Primary School, Bude

Fox Poem

A baby fox has just been born
in a snuggled bed all nice and warm.

The fox grows every day and night
getting stronger and stronger,
soon it's strong enough to stand.
Its fur starts to change to a bright auburn-brown.

Its eyes start to open and turn to a crystal-blue.
A few months later the fox is old enough
to hunt with its sharp teeth.

Finally the fox is old enough to leave its mother
and can care for itself.

Aimee Grace Mitchell (10)
Marhamchurch CE Primary School, Bude

Monster, Monster

Monster, monster in your bed
Monster, monster has gone red
Monster, monster gives you fright
Monster, monster is not a good sight

Witch, witch makes you itch
Witch, witch has a stitch
Witch, witch fell in a ditch
Witch, witch has a cat called Mitch

Ghost, ghost get a roast
Ghost, ghost need some toast?
Ghost, ghost get a rest
Ghost, ghost is so obsessed

Goblin, goblin is a freak
Goblin, goblin is not to seek
Goblin, goblin always reeks
Goblin, goblin lives in a peak

Snake, snake eat a rake
Snake, snake you're going to bake
Snake, snake for goodness sake
Snake, snake you always take

Moon, moon see you soon
Sun, sun on the run
Kerchi run, run we've got a gun
(And all the monsters run away).

Callum Heywood & Joshua Summers (11)
Marhamchurch CE Primary School, Bude

The Noisy Forest

I see the forest with lots of trees.
The beetles munch the dried-up leaves.
The trees whisper to one another.
The leaves scrunch underneath me.
The sun shines on the wet leaves.

Emma Kitchener (11)
Marhamchurch CE Primary School, Bude

The Noisy Super Jungle

The jungle is so noisy,
The trees whisper to me,
The sun glistens through the leaves,
The elephants stomp,
The giraffes chomp,
The monkeys swing through the trees.

Charlotte White (10)
Marhamchurch CE Primary School, Bude

The Magic Box

(Based on 'Magic Box' by Kit Wright)

I will put in my box . . .

the blazing blink of a Cyclops' eye,
the last concert of Beethoven
and the first songbird in spring,

the ear-splitting bang of a Christmas firework
and the final spin of the Catherine wheel.

I will put in the box . . .

an eleventh planet and a second sun,
a jockey in a spaceship
and an alien on a black stallion,

the dance of a firefly on a summer's night
and the soft tender touch of an autumn breeze.

My box is fashioned from cloud chocolate and spider silk and bronze,
with lion manes on the lid and puppy dogs in the corner.
Its hinges are made from Saturn's rings.

I shall glide in my box
like a bird in the sky
then land ashore on a hot sunny beach,
that is the colour of love.

Catherine Romney (8)
Modbury Primary School, Modbury

The Magic Box
(Based on 'Magic Box' by Kit Wright)

I will put in the box . . .

the two large horns of a fierce black rhino,
the last silk web from a black widow spider
and the first whisper of a teddy bear.

I will put in the box . . .

an eleventh planet and a twin Earth,
a footballer in a white spaceship
and an alien scoring goals.

I will put in the box . . .

a cool sun and a hot moon,
a hunter with shimmering dragon scales
and a dragon with a shotgun.

My box is fashioned from shimmering ice and sparkling silver
with transparent crystals on the lid and planets in the corners.
Its hinges are the sharp claws of a golden eagle.

I will sail on my box to the end of the Earth.

Kirsty Lock (9)
Modbury Primary School, Modbury

Bird In The Sky

Bird in the sky,
What do you see?
Wind throwing the clouds across the sky,
Ants doing the conga.

Bird in the sky,
What do you see?
Turtles surfing,
Fish teasing the seagulls,
Dolphins squealing as they backflip.

Tyler Gilley (9)
Modbury Primary School, Modbury

The Magic Box
(Based on 'Magic Box' by Kit Wright)

I will put in the box . . .

the last baby tooth to go from a 60-year-old adult,
a quarter moon and a half sun,
a monkey talking like a teddy.

I will put in the box . . .

an elephant with a large cowboy suit,
a cowboy decorated like an Indian elephant (yeeha!)
a teddy spitting like a llama.

I will put in my box . . .

Year 4 class looking like Narnia,
Narnia looking like Year 4 class,
Scooby-Doo! with seaweed all over him.

My box is fashioned from chocolate and purple sweetie wrappers,
with mint on the lid and Skittles in the corners.
Its hinges are made of fluffy clouds with a shepherd sky and
                                                    dragon claws.

I will fly on a Chinese dragon inside my box across the black
                                                    forests of Asia.

Hannah Brace (9)
Modbury Primary School, Modbury

Bird In The Sky

Bird in the sky,
What do you see?
The wind lobbing the clouds,
In a gymnastics competition.

Bird in the sky,
What do you see?
A hedgehog fast bowling for the England team.

Liam Twohig (8)
Modbury Primary School, Modbury

The Magic Box
(Based on 'Magic Box' by Kit Wright)

I will put in the box . . .

the first century of the Earth,
the last animal on the ark,
a pure, safe world for all the children.

I will put in the box . . .

a shape-shifting sun and a multicoloured star,
a witch riding a horse
and a cowboy rounding a cauldron.

My box is fashioned from burning red ruby and shimmering sapphire,
with spectacular moonstone on the lid and ancient secrets in the
                                                                  crouched corners.
Its hinges are piranhas' jaws, snapping as it shuts.

I shall fly around the world in my box
and land in the sea with 15 foot waves zooming above me
as I get washed ashore
to the sparkling sand, reflecting the sun.

Finlay Andrews (9)
Modbury Primary School, Modbury

The Magic Box
(Based on 'Magic Box' by Kit Wright)

I will put in the box . . .

the first blink of an eye,
the last roar of a tiger.

My box is fashioned from shining ice and gold
and different rainbow colours,
with shimmering fish on the lid and snowflakes in the corners.
Its hinges are tigers' claws.

Jake Harvey-Doddridge (9)
Modbury Primary School, Modbury

The Magic Box
(Based on 'Magic Box' by Kit Wright)

I will put in the box . . .

the proud summit of Mount Everest,
the last blink of an ancient mummy
and the first cry of a Roman emperor.

I will put in the box . . .

the core of Earth and a black hole,
a fourth lion on the England shirt
and a seventh stud on a football boot.

My box is fashioned from platinum and jade,
a splash of pale orange ocean on the lid
with a base made from love
and Latin wishes in the corners.
Its hinges are angel wings.

In my box I shall fly
across the English sky
to the land of the dinosaurs
where no one is forgotten.

Peter Blackler (9)
Modbury Primary School, Modbury

Bird In The Sky

Bird in the sky,
What do you see?
A squirrel racing up
And down the tree,
Fish showing off to the seagulls,
By surfing off the rooftops,
Bees buzzing across the road like darts.

Benjamin Teague (9)
Modbury Primary School, Modbury

The Magic Box
(Based on 'Magic Box' by Kit Wright)

I will put in the box . . .

the first drop of a rain cloud,
the last spark of a firework
and the moan of an Egyptian mummy.

I will put in the box . . .

a wizard with a shotgun,
a hunter with a magic staff
and a leprechaun hiding his clovers.

My box is fashioned from gold and bubble juice and velvet,
with the magic of the Grim Reaper on the lid
and silk wishes in the corners.
Its hinges are strawberry laces.

I shall sail in my box
underwater like a submarine.

Jade Birch (9)
Modbury Primary School, Modbury

Bird In The Sky

Bird in the sky,
What do you see?
Field mice playing rugby,
Snakes doing stunts on scooters,
Bees bellowing at other insects,
Rats playing rounders,
Spiders singing silly songs.

Bird in the sky,
What to you see?
Submarines bursting out the water,
Fish flipping funnily,
Planes soaring in the fluffy sky,
Clouds looking like funny faces.

Jack Sturton (8)
Modbury Primary School, Modbury

The Magic Box
(Based on 'Magic Box' by Kit Wright)

I will put in the box . . .

the first hour of sunrise
and the last curve of the shining moon.

I will put in the box . . .

a cool sun and a hot moon,
a carpenter running away
and a gingerbread man carving wood.

My box is fashioned from delicate sparkling webs and the
                                        pinkest sand and magic,
with shimmering sea on the lid and secret wishes in the corners.
Its hinges are carved from lions' claws.

I am going to drift in my box to a lucky island.

Elliott George (9)
Modbury Primary School, Modbury

Bird In The Sky

Bird in the sky, what do you see?
Jumbo jets howling through the sky.

Bird in the sky, what do you see?
Big Ben ringing and singing.

Bird in the sky, what do you see?
The Tower of London wobbling.

Bird in the sky, what do you see?
Bees whispering to one another -
London.

Adam Keates (9)
Modbury Primary School, Modbury

The Magic Box
(Based on 'Magic Box' by Kit Wright)

I will put in the box . . .

the first hop from an Australian kangaroo
and the last charge of a black rhinoceros.

I will put in the box . . .

a thirteenth month and a cheddar moon,
a dragon *catching* the robbers
and a policeman *rescuing the princess.*

My box is fashioned from pink candyfloss and rainbows,
with diamonds on the lid and rose rubies in the corners.
Its hinges are wizards' curly moustaches.

I will glide in a flaming aeroplane over the clearest turquoise sea
along to the magic land on a golden beach.

Angus West (9)
Modbury Primary School, Modbury

The Magic Box
(Based on 'Magic Box' by Kit Wright)

I will put in the box . . .

a glass sun and a nonagon moon,
a teacher swirling a magic horn
and a unicorn signing homework books.

My box is fashioned from electric waves and Indian spices and
                                                    warm sand
with emerald-green flowers on the lid and memories in the corner.
Its hinges are horns, sharp like needles.

Beth Wilson (9)
Modbury Primary School, Modbury

The Magic Box
(Based on 'Magic Box' by Kit Wright)

I will put in the box . . .

a thirteenth month and a triangular moon,
an angler painting rainbows on fish
and an artist catching a masterpiece!

I will put in the box . . .

three red wishes,
the last snowman in winter
and the first bulb of spring.

My box is fashioned from fluffy clouds and shepherds; sky
and snow as soft as feathers,
with sharp dragon claws on the lid
and carved unicorn horns in the corners.
Its hinges are stalagmites.

Billy Jones (9)
Modbury Primary School, Modbury

The Magic Box
(Based on 'Magic Box' by Kit Wright)

I will put in the box . . .

a purple moon with a green sun,
the last flame of an eclipse,
the first hour of every day.

My box is fashioned from human bones
and diamonds and golden steel,
with a sapphire on the lid
and a scarlet sunset in the corners.
Its hinges are two halves of the moon.

Jake Beer (9)
Modbury Primary School, Modbury

The Magic Box
(Based on 'Magic Box' by Kit Wright)

I will put in the box . . .

the last piece of treasure on an ancient pirate ship,
the first drop of rain for a parched desert.

I will put in the box . . .

my birthday with all the trimmings
the first autumn leaf and the last winter snowflake.

My box is fashioned from shimmering fairy dust
and precious wedding lace,
with marshmallows on the lid and Maltesers in the corners.
Its hinges are golden phoenix wings.

I will soar on a magic carpet over the sizzling golden sand
and settle under a palm tree, swaying like ribbons.

Jenny Grace (9)
Modbury Primary School, Modbury

The Magic Box
(Based on 'Magic Box' by Kit Wright)

I will put in the box . . .

five rainbow wishes spoken in Chinese,
the last word of a sister,
the first bark of a Jack Russell terrier.

I will put in the box . . .

366 leap days and a cuboid sun.

My box is fashioned from mint and paper and lightning,
with humming on the lid and dreams in the corners.
Its hinges are fangs from a deadly king cobra.

I shall float in my box and drift ashore on a sunshine beach.

Andrew Low (9)
Modbury Primary School, Modbury

The Magic Box
(Based on 'Magic Box' by Kit Wright)

I will put in the box . . .

the cackle of an ancient witch,
the blossom of an ever-growing cherry tree
and the swish of a buzzard soaring high up above.

I will put in the box . . .

a mimic mouth and a glass sun,
a dog walker with shining armour
and a knight with leads.

I will put in the box . . .

three wishes spoken in vain,
the pages of an invisible book
and the path of a shooting star.

I will put in the box . . .

the squawk of a parrot,
the call of a newborn badger
and the silence of a snowfall.

My box is fashioned from touch and amber and the Earth's core,
with the sound of bells on the lid and earwax in the corners.
Its hinges are the whisper of the wind.

I shall kayak in my box
over the clear turquoise water
then glide to shore
to swing with the orang-utans.

Tess Hemsi (9)
Modbury Primary School, Modbury

The Magic Box
(Based on 'Magic Box' by Kit Wright)

I will put in the box . . .

the sound of curtains drawing as the sunshine pours in,
the last petal falling from a gentle lily,
the first hour of the world beginning.

I will put in the box . . .

a fourth hand on the clock and a green moon,
a swallow back from its dangerous journey
and a welcome wave from the wild swirling ocean.

I will put into the box . . .

seven joyful colours of a rainbow,
a spring garden bursting with life,
a bronze leaf dancing in the autumn breeze.

My box is fashioned from deep blue sky and marshmallow clouds
and twinkling stars,
with glistening emeralds on the lid and clear white snowflakes in
the corners.
Its hinges are made from ruby crab shells that sparkle in the sunlight.

I will swim in my box through a turquoise sea with a school
of dolphins,
and arrive at a pale beach where I shall canter on
a dapple-grey pony.

Mary-Kate Dolley (8)
Modbury Primary School, Modbury

The Magic Box
(Based on 'Magic Box' by Kit Wright)

I will put in the box . . .

three promises whispered as an oath,
the last sweet scent of a rose
and the first kiss of a bride.

I will put in the box . . .

a cube-shaped sun,
a double moon
and Superman in cuddly fur.

My box is fashioned from tulip chains
and shimmering sunshine and clear turquoise-blue oceans,
with love hearts on the lid
and jolly songs in the corner.
Its hinges are slithering water slides.

I shall soar through my box
over the glistening sea
then land in Hawaii
on a gorgeous sunshine beach.

Anna Lee (8)
Modbury Primary School, Modbury

The Magic Box
(Based on 'Magic Box' by Kit Wright)

I will put in the box . . .

the last tick of an ancient clock,
the first bark of a newborn puppy,
every special day, and the special days to come.

I will put in the box . . .

a 25th hour and a banana moon,
an ugly pirate dressed as a fairy
and a fairy with a parrot, perched on her shoulder.

My box is fashioned from the deepest, blackest sky
and a gleaming moon,
with a crimson sun on the lid and sparkling stars in the corners.
Its hinges are the excited ferns of a Christmas tree
at the rustling of wrapping paper.

I will zoom through the turquoise sea on my box
and reach the golden sands with the animals,
where I will live in paradise.

Cecily Edwards (9)
Modbury Primary School, Modbury

The Magic Box

I will put in the box . . .

three light breaths of a Chinese dragon,
the last whisper of an Egyptian king,
the first teardrop of a new baby.

I will put in the box . . .

an invisible sun and hidden moon,
a dolphin shooting out the water,
a dart piercing through the sky.

I will put in the box . . .

a swish of a silk curtain swirling in the breeze,
the Atlantic Ocean
as it swallows a boat into its angry depths.

My box is fashioned from ice and fire and dark magic,
with crocodile tongues on the lid and shadows in the corners.
Its hinges are unicorn bones, magically glowing.

I will soar over the Grand Canyon on my box,
the wind pushing me back,
while the sun bakes my shoulders.

Joe Berry (8)
Modbury Primary School, Modbury

The Magic Box
(Based on 'Magic Box' by Kit Wright)

I will put in the box . . .

the searching sounds of an orca whale,
the first glimpse of a pirate ship
and the last stretch of a deckchair.

I will put in my box . . .

a thirteenth month and a double Christmas,
the favourite chats with my teddy bear
who I've treasured since I was a baby.

My box is fashioned from blood-red rubies
and spinning whirlwinds around a scorching sun,
with jingling bells on the lid
and unicorns' manes in the corners.
Its hinges are the jaws of a wise dragon with sapphire teeth.

I will roller blade on my box to Antarctica,
past the fluffy white polar bears,
feathery penguins and barking seals,
to gaze alone at a rainbow sunset.

Kiera-Louise Snell (8)
Modbury Primary School, Modbury

The Magic Box
(Based on 'Magic Box' by Kit Wright)

I will put in the box . . .

a 25th hour and a blue moon
the last cuddle of a favourite aunt
and the first word of a toddler.

My box is fashioned from gold and silver
and the whistling of the wind,
with glittering stars on the lid
and rubies in the corners.
Its hinges are made from crystal-clear glass.

I will fly in my box
on the whispering wind,
to fantasy lands -
the place of dreams.

Beth Holgate (8)
Modbury Primary School, Modbury

Volcano

Volcano,
Liquid hot, scarlet ferocious head,
Only to annihilate,
Feeling the need to whirl out of control!

Hazardous volcano,
Sense to kill,
As dangerous as a murdering tornado in an over-populated area!
The volcano is an inferno!

Its lava is as red as a tiger coat
Then *boom!*
The deafening eruption of lava exploding into the air.
Finishing off with red ruby lava rocks all over the Earth!

Matthew Meade (11)
Ninfield CE Primary School, Ninfield

Tiger

Tiger paces elegantly around his cage.
Slows, then halts and peers outside,
His eager eyes remember what they had once experienced.

The open world,
No bars to hold him back.
Feeling the leaves crunching delightfully
Welcoming him home.

He spots prey!
Swallowing the ground beneath his feet
He snatches it,
Grabbing the meat, sinking his teeth.
Tiger feels blood running down his chin.
He is home!

Sound of bars rattling snap him back to reality.
Dinner time.
His dream is gone.

Abbie Nixon (11)
Ninfield CE Primary School, Ninfield

The Sea

Calm sea like a kitten fast asleep,
Fluffy white horse riding at the gnarled rocks,
Sun oozing through the sand
Whilst trees sway in the musical wind.
Waves wail at their parents,
Trying to find directions home.
Angry like a bolt of lightning
Brewing up a thunderstorm,
Broken branches crash huts;
All that remains - salty smell.

Gemma Connor (11)
Ninfield CE Primary School, Ninfield

Volcano

Volcano,
Corpulent, encrusted, boiling ring, surrounding the summit.
Scolding volcanic fluid approaches.
The danger is brutal,
Big dome-shaped figure explodes.
Ground shakes and howls in trepidation.
Rock turns durable,
It squeaks heartily.
The ferocious hiss of the oozing lava,
Expensive marble and other rock now coated in thick liquid block.
Volcano fires out a bulky grunt of terror.
People apprehend the volcanoes' resentment,
Finally, silence is obtained,
The volcano is inactive.

Jules Siviter (11)
Ninfield CE Primary School, Ninfield

The Sea's Senses

People trespass inquisitive,
Unable to seek out what will emerge.
The sea opens its blue tongue
And sucks them in.

The sea is stained,
Blood is left.
Anger surrounds the sea,
Whilst sharks chuckle.

The sea is distressed,
Pollution has done its job.
Land is attacked,
The sea's rage has destroyed the world,
Until only land and sea are left.

Zak Barton (11)
Ninfield CE Primary School, Ninfield

Endangered Tiger

Greenish-grey eyes sparkle for hope
Pin-needle whiskers twitch in alarm
Soft innocent tears flutter down her cheeks
Black fuzzy stripes shake for fear of harm.

She wants freedom
Pouncing legs to seize her prey
Longing for the jungle
Wanting company
She wants to hear animals squeal
Dreaming of smelling her prey
Worried and wanting to run away
So she can be happy
For the rest of her life.

Rebekka Abel (10)
Ninfield CE Primary School, Ninfield

The Sea . . .

The sea is dyed a glistening, sparkling deep blue.
A home for magnificent, breathtaking sea life,
Home for all types of amazing crustaceans,
Repetitive anemones elegantly planting on the cracking rocks.

Forever the salty void remains,
A soft, yet awesomely forceful wave splashes legs
Whilst a warm, comforting breeze tickles
Relaxingly . . .
The sun bursts out burning rays, frazzling the dried out starfishes,
Dazed by the lack of moisture,
Frothy waves wash away the sun's anger,
The sea's goal, achieved, world peace,
Earning the name of Miss World!

Hallam Earl (10)
Ninfield CE Primary School, Ninfield

The Scream

Lonely cold eyes.
Hands muffle sounds to ears.
Frustrated, he.
Veins urge upon his forehead.
While beads of sweat crawl down his nose.

Screeching echoes.
Down a tunnel,
Rancid bodies -
The smell wafts upon his nostrils.

The river is a blue roller coaster
Weaving towards oceans.
Memories,
Blood river,
Bodies flow in blood river,
Salty water drenches his taste buds.

Prickly wood scars his pale hands,
While beetles and spiders creep down.

Vanya Askew (10)
Ninfield CE Primary School, Ninfield

The Tiger

Fiery red ruby eyes,
Soft and silky lava-coated fur,
Jagged claws,
Razor-sharp teeth coated in blood,
Padded feet feeling the sponge and crisp leaves,
Prickly wet grass,
The cold wind blowing through his sleek fur,
When he digs his sharp teeth into a piece of deer as if it were alive,
Its nose is hard and scaly like a snake's body.

Oliver Charles Greene (11)
Ninfield CE Primary School, Ninfield

The Volcano Wrath

Volcano.
Can't immobilise the sticky past inside it.
It suddenly erupts in a confused feeling,
Letting hatred win,
The hot lava spits and screams in agony
As it soars through the air.
Remaining lava crawls across the land,
Like a caterpillar in search of fluorescent light.
Trees are flies caught in a web,
Impossible to escape from the predator that awaits it.
Lava burns anything in its way
Causing destruction and havoc
To the creatures in its path.
A thick veil of black smoke darkens the land.
One sniff and death is upon you.
The force of the beast is diminutive.
The once uncontrollable animal stops.
Volcano!

Mohammad Bourner (11)
Ninfield CE Primary School, Ninfield

Volcano

As fuming as a mother
Being wound up by a naughty child.
Huge encrusted mouth spits out fiery rocks
And deadly lava as hot as the sun's centre.

Monstrous explosion like an earthquake
Irritates the furious volcano further.
Shouts in fury causing rocks
And acid to shower the land below
Slowly smoke disappears and
Volcano calms and relaxes.

Sophie Roller (10)
Ninfield CE Primary School, Ninfield

Tiger

Tiger,
Nose of slime
Sniffing sparse surroundings,
Stringy wire whiskers twitch
At interruptions and noises,
Camouflaged striped fur
Rustles in the air-conditioned cage.
Reluctant paws paddle
Unhappily looking for an escape
From uprooting concrete.

Tiger,
Photogenic face,
Full of angry attitude,
Moist tongue,
Helping roar its way to freedom.

Tiger,
Trees comfort,
Cuddle and brush,
Against his
Joyful fur.
Eagle eyes
Scan nature-full forest,
Hoping to fill him with joy -
Mouth-watering meat.

Tiger,
Full of freedom,
Joy and happiness -
At last.

Ellie Whiting (11)
Ninfield CE Primary School, Ninfield

Danger

Leaping lava lunged at eroding rocks
The air was dirty with smoke and dust that floated through
                                       the polluted air
The volcano dilated, sending blistering rocks soaring over the tiny
                                village and colliding with houses
The petrified screams of the fleeing villagers filled the air with fear
With hatred the wind blew the sweltering lava closer to the
                                               scared villagers
Trees reaching over caught fire and fell crashing through houses
The fire was the disaster as it raced down the line of houses
Lava hotter than boiling water covered and preserved everything
Everything that lived or stood was gone.

Tommy Hart (11)
Ninfield CE Primary School, Ninfield

Animals Going Mad

There's a dog chasing my cat
And my cat's chasing a rat,
This all happened while I was putting on my hat,
Oh no! I think my cat got the rat,
He's looking a little fat.
Where is my dog? Is he still chasing my cat?
Oh no! I almost sat on my cat.
Oh my cat! Stop playing with my hat!
Oh no! My dog and cat and rat have gone mad!

Alicia Bowers (9)
Ormer House Preparatory School, Alderney

The Unwanted Genie

Crash, bang and a clap of thunder,
What was that I wonder?
We followed the noise all over the place
Then we finally found the trace.

It was a tiny lamp, it was moving all about,
We picked it up and with a great almighty *whoosh,*
Out came a beautiful genie, then there was a loud *sshh!*

We were quiet; she said, 'My name is Micha,
I am a great genie, I can grant your wish.'
The first wish was very exciting,
For a magic carpet as fast as lightning.

We flew up high over the town,
Then with a *whoosh* came swooping down.
We fell into a clump of trees
And hurt our elbows and our knees.

Our joy had turned to anger and fear
And wished for the genie to disappear.

Stephanie Dale (11)
Ormer House Preparatory School, Alderney

Mr Black

Once there was a dragon that stole a big fat wagon,
Then everyone got so, so scared they went to go and whack him.

This very naughty dragon actually had a name
And it was Mr Black.
Mr Black was black and smelly like some blackcurrant jelly.

The villagers did not find him,
It really was a shame.
The dragon felt so, so sorry and did not take the blame.

Joseph Stanley (9)
Ormer House Preparatory School, Alderney

Man's Best Friend

Big nose
small toes

Long tail
I'm male

Smelly fur
don't purr

Loves bones
not phones

Soft ears
no fears

Sharp teeth
eats beef

Cat hater
sleep later

Man's best friend!

Lewis Wells (11)
Pensans Community Primary School, Penzance

Rivers

Splashing, racing
raging for the sea
down the stream
crashing and flashing
jumping up and down
swishing and swirling
bending round corners
sliding up the bank
then down the bank
and into the deep blue sea.

Chris McKee Rogers (11)
Pensans Community Primary School, Penzance

What Am I?

Arm licker,
leg cocker,
grass sniffer,
cat chaser.

Door scratcher,
sleep lover,
bone chewer,
ball catcher.

Beach runner,
tail wagger,
pawprint maker,
family friend.

A: my dog.

Katie Birchall-Kells (10)
Pensans Community Primary School, Penzance

I Am What?

Seaweed eater
sea lover
tail flipper
wave rider.

Rock sitter
hair lover
nearly human
breathtaking singer.

I'm a . . .
Mermaid!

Lucy Elizabeth Barker (11)
Pensans Community Primary School, Penzance

Who Am I?

Dark hair,
caring friend,
hoop earrings,
choco eyes.

Dark eyebrows,
short 'n' slim,
brain bulging,
creative drawer.

Craft worker,
English lover,
high heels-aholic,
Chocolate mad.

Who is she?
My best friend for life!
Katie Kells.

Bethany Blewett (10)
Pensans Community Primary School, Penzance

Wayne Rooney

Wayne Rooney is super fast
his shots are a blast
skill is his middle name.

A footballer he became
Man United is his team.

When he comes on the pitch
the crowd scream
he is a penalty shooter

and a good booter.
Come on Rooney
we're all going looney.

Brandon Bugden (11)
Pensans Community Primary School, Penzance

The Place I Love To Go

I know a place where I like to go,
It is very nice, I love it so,
It has lots of trees and leaves,
Please come and see it with me.

It has a pool,
A big pool with all my imagination,
This is a place I would like to go to.

Jodie Robinson (10)
Pensans Community Primary School, Penzance

Killer Whale

Black and white
fish killer
ocean wrecker
deep sea killer
seal chaser
meat eater
sea stalker
slow killer.

Chris Hocking (10)
Pensans Community Primary School, Penzance

Killer Whale

Seal killer
Fish seizer
Blood halver
Sea diver
Group hunter.

Sam Skinner (11)
Pensans Community Primary School, Penzance

Outside

I really like nature,
The shades of green,
It's the loveliest sight,
I have ever seen.

The trees are so pretty,
With animals inside,
That's one of the good things,
About the outside.

The rivers are beautiful,
They look so alive!
And all of the fishes,
They dip and they dive.

All different weathers,
Rain, wind and sun,
No matter what the weather,
You can always have fun!

Well, that's enough for now,
I hope you liked my poem,
I'm starting on another one,
I'd better get going!

Alice Chaplin (11)
Pensans Community Primary School, Penzance

Racing - Haiku

Not a race for gold
But a race for second place
Maybe even bronze.

Cory Austwick (10)
Pensans Community Primary School, Penzance

Our World

Our world it is a beautiful space,
Which homes the whole of the human race,
With ocean, land, wet and dry,
And I promise this poem isn't a lie.

The forest is a beautiful space,
With loads of plants all over the place,
Some animals live within the trees,
Or bury themselves under fallen leaves.

The ocean is a beautiful space,
Which homes many fish such as plaice,
Coral stuck to the ocean floor,
But the sea it homes much, much more.

The world it is a beautiful space,
Which homes the whole of the human race,
But if we don't look after it, it will soon be gone,
A dim lightbulb which had once shone.

Owen Donald Fellows (10)
Pensans Community Primary School, Penzance

Auntie May

I visited my auntie May
Just last Sunday
She baked a roast
It turned out like toast
That was the end of my Sunday

The very next week
I visited the antique
She cooked a casserole
I puked in a bowl
Don't think I'll visit her next week!

Sophie Weeks (11)
Pensans Community Primary School, Penzance

My Magic Box
(Based on 'Magic Box' by Kit Wright)

I will put in my box . . .

a drop in the ocean,
a ton of lava jumping around,
a dog as fast as a cheetah.

I will put in my box . . .

dolphins jumping through a hoop,
two birds singing in a tree in the dark night,
a dog howling the night away.

I will put in my box . . .

a shining sun shining on everything and everyone,
a snowy top of Mount Everest,
a frog on a lily pad.

Nick Herring (11)
Pensans Community Primary School, Penzance

The England Team

The England team are alright,
If you switch on the light.
Peter Crouch is so tall,
He can see over the wall.

Aaron Lennon running down the wing,
Wayne Rooney on the swing.
Michael Owen banging in the goals,
Making the net have lots of holes.

Daniel Paul Ferris (10)
Pensans Community Primary School, Penzance

My Dream

In my dream I saw a sunbeam,
It looked so magical,
I could hear the drops of a stream,
With a beam of sun reflecting on it,
With a heart shape of angelfish huddled together.

Hannah Maddern (10)
Pensans Community Primary School, Penzance

Crab - Haiku

Big clattering crab
Big, hungry and snappy crab
Pinches little crabs.

Asa Paddock (8)
Port Isaac CP School, Port Isaac

The Crab - Haiku

The ginormous crab
snip snip in the deep rock pool
I saw it nip her.

Courtney Summers (8)
Port Isaac CP School, Port Isaac

The Sun - Haiku

The shimmering sun
is boiling and can burn you
does not always shine.

Harry Hambly (8)
Port Isaac CP School, Port Isaac

The Boat - Haiku

The massive blue boat
Has a big noisy engine
Holds loads of people!

Sam Lorimer (7)
Port Isaac CP School, Port Isaac

The Crab - Haiku

The big vicious crab.
Don't go near it in the pool
Or else it will bite.

Liam Murray Strout (8)
Port Isaac CP School, Port Isaac

The Crab - Haiku

The hard pinchy crab
can be hard and dangerous
watch out for his claws!

Tom Penny (8)
Port Isaac CP School, Port Isaac

The Crab Curse - Haiku

My vicious French crab
kills its own little babies.
I hate my French crab.

Sinead Tiddy (8)
Port Isaac CP School, Port Isaac

Old Crab - Haiku

The old ugly crab
needs to get a new girlfriend
and a new haircut.

Gus Houston (9)
Port Isaac CP School, Port Isaac

Sunglasses - Haiku

Red cool sunglasses,
My red sparkling sunglasses
From the new red shop.

Holly Hambly (8)
Port Isaac CP School, Port Isaac

The Icicle

A delicate chrysalis embedded in snow.
Winter's gem compound and sown
Woven with a drop of water
Glistening in the silver light
Lost in time for evermore!

A sparkling chrysalis that hangs from the moon
A sickle
A trickle
A beam of light

Until a shiver it shall stay
Then the sun comes out and it melts away
A delicate teardrop easily broken
An icicle so precious is easily forsaken.

Gaia Hancock (11)
Punnets Town CP School, Heathfield

Seven Things In The Fairies' Cave!

A silent squishy moon waiting to be cuddled once more,
A bottle of monkey's mischief trying to push its way out,
A devil's cauldron, waiting for people to stir in,
A secret star full of gentle wishes,
A never-ending wish from a devil, waiting to be granted,
A chuckle from a sweet baby, captured in a fairy's dream,
An angel's heart releasing children's wishes . . .

Chloe Chidsey (10)
Ramsbury Primary School, Ramsbury

Six Things Found In A Wrestler's Apartment

A big bully sledgehammer waiting to batter the brains out of any
                                                          barmy person,
A Wrestle Mania 21 poster that doesn't exist,
A silver shiny belt ready to defend once more,
The memory of three Royal Rumble winners in a rivalry,
A never-ending story of the Olympic gold medallist Kurt Angle,
The outline of the most amazing victory in WWE history.

Elliot Rai (11)
Ramsbury Primary School, Ramsbury

Six Things Found In A Chicken's Handbag

A magic door leading to a forbidden land
A voodoo doll,
A pink ballerina chicken stolen from Marshmallow Town,
A bottle of time captured in the moment,
An unspun sock from a pig's laundry
And an everlasting lipstick.

Tara Colsell-Hawes (11)
Ramsbury Primary School, Ramsbury

I Should Like To . . .

I should like to meet a glorious warrior elf
And become one of their heroic race.
I should like to ride an imperial dragon of my own
And slay all the evil in the world.

I should like to see gold dragon fire rush out of my hands
And control the mystic light and dark.
I would like to stop the sun from dying
And taste the black magic of an ancient mage.

I should like to lead the world to prosperity
And convert a wraith.
I should like to identify the secrets of the universe
And manipulate the gods of the world.

Jamie Goodhew (11)
Ramsbury Primary School, Ramsbury

My Likes And Dislikes

I like . . .

A tremendous kestrel, gliding above,
A beautiful crystal-white dove,
Two fighting badgers, scuttling around
And wriggling worms, slithering on the ground.

I dislike . . .

Deadly pollution, harming all life,
A hunter causing strife,
Death to all the urban foxes
And animals trapped in boxes.

William Ballard (11)
Ramsbury Primary School, Ramsbury

I Like To Hear . . .

The sound of a stallion galloping through a buttercup field,
the rattle from a baby's toy as it falls into open air,
the rough sea crash against the strong rocks,
ticking from a clock as silence arrives,
the grass swaying in the sunshine with a slight breeze . . .

I don't like to hear . . .

The blistering gale lashing on the cracked ground,
thunder and lightning smashing in the black clouds,
a gun going off then a sudden bang on the ground,
the sound of a glass breaking with a mysterious echo in
                                  the background . . .

Imogene Knight (11)
Ramsbury Primary School, Ramsbury

I Would Like To See . . .

A black stallion galloping,
A sunset shining gloriously,
A snowflake on the window sill,
A mysterious story oozing with life,
A deadly viper's laugh,
A queen's whisper,
A magical unicorn.

I would not like to see . . .
A start of a storm,
A deadly traffic jam,
A scarecrow who was alive,
A dead body awoken from the dead,
A sad man screeching with laughter . . .

Anya Milner (11)
Ramsbury Primary School, Ramsbury

Four Things Found Under A Fairy's Wing

A pink unicorn from the top
of a tip of a mountain,

A sack full of money
from the deepest blue sea.

A cupboard full of sweets
from the white shiny cloud

And a special sparkle
from the moonlight.

Ellen Little (11)
Ramsbury Primary School, Ramsbury

Six Items From An Elf's Bag

The never-ending pearls dripping from a unicorn's mane,
The sun and the moon sparkling furiously,
The Devil's heart pumping terrifyingly,
The magic from a pixie's wand,
The love of the world trapped forever,
The frozen tears of Pluto.

Georgina Perkins (11)
Ramsbury Primary School, Ramsbury

Five Things Found In An Eskimo's Coat!

A genie's lamp for a hopeless boy.
A black heart from the Devil himself.
A pot of gold from the end of the rainbow.
A unicorn's horn.
A hyena's laugh captured in minutes.

Stephanie Milne (11)
Ramsbury Primary School, Ramsbury

A Place Rhyming Poem

Found a cleaner
In Argentina.

Found a bun
In Changchun.

Found a hand
In England.

Found a spanner
In Ghana.

Found a piece of bacon
In Interlaken.

Found a vest
In Keywest.

Found some bling
In Beijing.

Found a pan
In Durban.

Found a Ford
In Fjord.

Found a hare
In Harare.

Found a palaver
In Java.

Found some foam
In Rome.

Found a bongo
In Mongo.

Maia Pearce (11)
Ramsbury Primary School, Ramsbury

The Playground

As the double doors fly open,
the monkeys all pour in.
The raging battlefield worsens,
the venue is laden with din.

The troops march forward,
across the manic plain.
Bullies circle innocent scholars,
defending, but still receiving pain.

Girls skip merrily,
oblivious to the pitch.
Footballs flying overhead,
(boys don't get the glitch).

Dinner ladies serve food,
fit for only hogs.
rotten radish, gravy granules
and curried chilli dogs.

Playtime is over,
the field is empty once more.
They're all locked in stuffy rooms,
to them these times are chores.

George Martin-Johnson (10)
Ramsbury Primary School, Ramsbury

My Mum

My mum is a hot oven,
My mum is an open door,
She's going back and forward,
She's as soft as a teddy bear,
My mum is busy as a bee.

Emma Falla (10)
St Andrew's Primary School, St Andrew's

My Cat Binks

My cat is as ginger as a gingerbread man
He runs as fast as he can
He has white paws
And very sharp claws
And that's why I like him so much

I love him lots and lots
And he has spots
His tail is furry
And it's very curly
And his nose is bright pink.

Jessica Dean (10)
St Andrew's Primary School, St Andrew's

Fairtrade

Round the world poor people live,
Eating rice through a sieve,
They work so hard to keep alive,
Collecting honey from a bee's hive,
Coco pods with coco beans,
The tastiest that's ever seen,
Food in those countries can be made,
If you go out and buy Fairtrade!

Phoebe Morgan (10)
St Andrew's Primary School, St Andrew's

My Friend - Christopher Scowen

He's as funny as a clown,
He's as fast as a rocket,
He wouldn't hurt a fly,
He's as clever as the Internet,
He's as bright as a banana.

Giles Quigley (9)
St Andrew's Primary School, St Andrew's

The Writer Of This Poem
(Based on 'The Writer of this Poem' by Roger McGough)

The writer of this poem is . . .
As sturdy as a tree
As clever as an owl
As determined as can be.

As dainty as a daisy
As sneaky as a spy
As cheeky as a baby elephant
As fluffy as a cloud in the sky.

As calm as a sunset
As little as a mouse
As quiet as a watch's tick
As still as an empty house.

'The writer of this poem
Never ceases to amaze
She's one in a million billion
Or so the poem says!'

Freya McLaren (8)
St Andrew's Primary School, St Andrew's

Star Wars Acrostic Poem

S tarfighters zooming past the glistening stars
T rying to reach their destination
A round the galaxy defeating Sith
R ed ones, yellow ones, different ships

W hizzing speeders on Endou
A t-at on Hoth
R ed lightsabers for the Sith
S oon the Jedi will bring peace.

Oscar Anderson (10)
St Andrew's Primary School, St Andrew's

The Writer Of This Poem
(Based on 'The Writer of this Poem' by Roger McGough)

The writer of this poem is . . .
As tall as a giraffe,
As shy as a mouse coming out for tea,
As sweet as a packet of delicious fudge,
As cheeky as a monkey.

As bright as a new moon,
As intelligent as an owl,
As adventurous as a fox coming out at night,
As calm as a hibernating hedgehog.

As neat as a display
As funky as New Look
As happy as a rescued puppy,
As popular as Take That.

'The writer of this poem
Never ceases to amaze
She's one in a million billion,
Or so the poem says!'

Beatrice Morgan (8)
St Andrew's Primary School, St Andrew's

Free

When you look around
You see a world very hurt
And in places wrong,
But if I work and try my hardest
The wrongs could become
Right.

I want to fight for justice
To grant the freedom we were given
The freedom that seems to have vanished.
Through our own lack of forgiveness,
Through our own lack of apologies,
Through our own fears.

Come join me to fight for justice,
Come join me to fight for freedom,
Come join me on a journey,
To change the future of mankind.

When you look at the world around us
You see people who are lonely,
But when you turn around again
You see smiling faces.
Come you smiling people, come
Help me to get justice.
Come join me to fight for justice,
Come join me to fight for freedom,
Come join me on a journey,
To change the future of mankind.

Eleanor Greenwood (11)
St Joseph's RC Primary School, Aldershot

Deadly Divorce

One deadly word that just breaks a family apart,
Breaking a lot of people's hearts,
All of that heartbreak,
That you have to take,
Why did people make such a thing as
Deadly divorce?

You hear them on the phone,
All that screams to you are unknown,
You want Mum,
You wand Dad,
You wish you just had
Both of them together,
Grey weather,
Whenever that memory appears,
You always shed tears,
Why did people make such a thing as
Deadly divorce?

You have to hear
All the horrible things they say about each other,
I think it has now been a year,
All the time you had to comfort your little brother,
Why do they have to fight?
Why can't they just talk?
Bellowing and screaming is such a fright.
Why did they make such a thing as
Deadly divorce?

You wish and dream
For all of us to be happy,
You beam,
Could you make it happen?

Emily Jones (11)
St Joseph's RC Primary School, Aldershot

Footy

Flowing through your fingers, flowing through your toes,
Your mother always says to you, *don't muddy your clothes,*
The beautiful game,
Isn't quite everyone's name,
But when you come up to deliver that final pass,
You always know you've got the class.

If you're the rock that doesn't roll,
You always put in your heart and soul,
You're always giving the opposition the eye,
You just zoom past as defenders fly by.
The crowd give you drive as they cheer on,
Your manager shouting from the touchline - *come on!*

If you nearly score, but hit the bar,
You come so close, but yet so far,
Football is great for everyone,
Especially when you're in the sun,
You have to use the full length of the pitch,
You needn't find the golden snitch.

When you are off and go down the tunnel,
You feel you want to evaporate through a funnel,
You jump into an early bath,
Maybe it's time for you to take a different path,
You can't afford to commit that foul,
Unfortunately now it's time to say ciâo!

Matthew Hutchinson (11)
St Joseph's RC Primary School, Aldershot

Marshmallows

Soft and squishy,
Pink and warm,
Nice and sticky,
Eat some more.

Let's make some smores,
With a warm marshmallow,
The chocolate pours,
The crackers are browny-yellow.

It melts in your mouth,
It's sugary sweet,
Scream and shout,
'Let's all eat!'

Lovely in cocoa,
Nice and warm,
Makes us go loco!
Makes us feel nice and warm!

Marshmallows can be pink,
Marshmallows can be white,
Marshmallows are the best I think,
But then chocolate might,
But nothing beats a marshmallow,
All pink ones, white ones, even yellow.

Sadie Taylor (11)
St Joseph's RC Primary School, Aldershot

Music

Music can be very loud,
Or even very quiet,
Music can be catchy,
Or even very dull!

Music can be very fun,
You can jump around and dance,
Music can be a huge excitement,
Making up your own tunes!

Music can be very fun
Is what I'm trying to say,
For some, music can be a bore,
But nobody hates music, I'm sure!

Mollie Spindler (10)
St Joseph's RC Primary School, Aldershot

Me

Dancing diva
Singing star
Footy queen
This *is* me!

Arty person
Homework hater
Person lover
This *is* me!

Cheeky monkey
Veggie hater
Fashion lover
This *is* me!

Georgia Carpenter (11)
St Joseph's RC Primary School, Aldershot

A Complicated World

The place we live in is a convoluted world
Full of lies and riddles I just can't understand
People being patriotic for no cause
People forever making wars
What happened to peace?
Why can't everyone decease?

Why do people try to fight?
Why can't people end this plight?
When people take justice to another
They sometimes sink as low as the other
What happened to peace?
Why can't people decease?

I don't understand this world
Maybe these riddles will unfurl
We will see until then
I'm trapped in a complicated world!

Hamish Radford Ross (10)
St Joseph's RC Primary School, Aldershot

I, The River

I run on through night and day,
always ready knowing the way,
seeing through eddies, bends and falls,
smashing off rocks, sides and walls.
Under bridges, through the town,
to the country, people around.
I don't want to hang around,
I will go and hear the sound,
go to see their flailing lock
flying around off the rocks
and see them wrestle, dance and flee,
never nearing close to thee.
And now I join their club with glee,
I am now part of the sea.

Pierre Le Poidevin (11)
St Martin's Primary School, St Martin's

Werewolf

We're standing in the graveyard,
my best friend Doddy begins to whine,
I look perplexed at her,
but then the silver clouds begin to part
and the full moon starts to shine.

'Come on!' I yell, 'quick let's run,'
but it's too late,
Doddy is standing transfixed
at the graveyard gate.

A horrid ripping sound,
as her clothes fall off,
she looks at me pleadingly
as she begins to cough.

Hair begins to sprout on her frail body,
fangs and claws appear,
I run away
and as I look back
I see growling snarling Doddy.

I run without a backward look,
while all I can hear is
the pounding of my heart,
splashing of my footsteps,
the babbling of the brook.

As the clock strikes midnight
I hear a dreadful howl
and to add to my fear
dogs start to bark
and cats begin to yowl.

I hear pounding from behind,
I know she's chasing me,
I'm absolutely petrified,
as terrified as can be.

I fall and stumble,
feel hot breath on my neck,
I know all's not well
as I tumble down,
down into the depth . . .

of Hell.

Joanna Richardson (10)
St Martin's Primary School, St Martin's

Rainbow

A rainbow appears.
A beautiful, sparkling rainbow appears.
A rainbow that nothing can beat.
It shines,
a colourful blur,
yet so neat.
The rainbow shines.
A bright, magical rainbow shines.
It arches,
over the harbour,
over me.
The rainbow sparkles,
like colourful dust - that's what I see.
It sparkles.
An amazing, arching rainbow sparkles.
It gently, slowly starts to fade
the rainbow that the weather made.
A rainbow fades.
A beautiful, arching, glittering,
glistening, amazing, colourful rainbow fades.

Stephanie Bisson (11)
St Martin's Primary School, St Martin's

The Creeper

Round every corner he will lurk
Invisible in the thick brown murk
The bright fish flicker and flash
As the creeper makes a dash
The school of fish try to flee
As three's a great chase to be

The tiny fish race away in fright
As the ugly beast prepares to fight
Fish swim frantically under rocks
As the time of life tick-tocks
The creeper swims past, not pursuing his prey
Disappointed as he's had no lunch that day

The fish swim out with great relief
Only to be greeted with great grief
As the creeper had come again
To send the fish down death lane
They all dart away in despair
Overcome by this nightmare

The bloodthirsty creeper had come back
Determined for a tasty snack
He gobbled up everything in his path
And finished off with a great big laugh
However this was his final say
As an even bigger fish made him pay

This was the creeper's final swish
As there is always a bigger fish!

Tomos A Geraint Ap Siôn (11)
St Martin's Primary School, St Martin's

The River

The darkness of the silent river
Makes every creature near it shiver
And amongst the ink and murk
Evil-hearted spirits lurk
They wait and wait for hour upon hour
Until something comes that they can devour
Slowly and strangely, the river flows
Where does it all go? Well . . .
Nobody knows . . .

With ten sharp teeth and silver back
The spirits glide through water black
And hiding, motionless, in the ink
They leap at the deer that comes to drink
Soon all that is left are antlers and bones
Lying in the mud with the grass and stones
Slowly and strangely, the river flows
Where does it all go? Well . . .
Nobody knows . . .

Many miles on from the old oak tree
The river opens up and flows into the sea
A wave engulfs the spirits that glide
And brings them in and out with the tide
But one man knows what the spirits would do
If they stayed alive in the ocean blue
Slowly and strangely, the river flows
Where does it all go? Well . . .
King Neptune knows . . .

Sarah Keirle (10)
St Martin's Primary School, St Martin's

The Hare And The Tortoise

The hare stood, heart pulsating
On the start line, waiting, waiting
For days he had prepared for this race
To lose, it would be a disgrace.

The tortoise whereas, was extremely calm
And to the hare's great alarm
Did not seem scared about defeat
In fact, he looked rather upbeat.

For the tortoise knew, what the hare did not
'Cause the hare, (he didn't know a lot)
Slow and steady wins the race
And the hare would go off at a blistering pace!

The sound of the start gun banged through the air
Starting the race between tortoise and hare
Sprinting, the hare rushed down the lane
The tortoise thought he was insane!

And indeed, he was perfectly right
And to his absolute delight
The hare, who was tired, sat down for a rest
Thinking that he was easily best.

However, he soon began to doze
And when he eventually arose
The tortoise was on the finishing straight
It appeared that the hare had woken too late!

So he jumped up and bolted round the bend
But the tortoise was already at the end
Jumping triumphantly like a winner could
Jumping triumphantly like a winner should!

There is a message to this tale
That if you do not want to fail
Slow and steady is the key
Slow and steady to victory!

George Mason (11)
St Martin's Primary School, St Martin's

The Old Oak

My bark has broken,
My sap has wept,
Like the tears I've never kept.

My layers have loosened,
My leaves are lost,
I suppose the years have general costs.

My flowers have blossomed,
My branches have wired,
Oh how much I've been admired.

My trunk has travelled,
My roots have run,
I remember the scorching sun.

My wrinkles are wrinkled,
My cracks have collided
And soon my fate will be decided.

The ivy is increasing,
The weeds are winding,
Soon I will not see the young children riding.

But so very soon my worries will cease
And travel up,
To the sky of peace,
Where I will never need to be stressed . . .

So I'm going now for my continuous rest.

Georgina Prow (11)
St Martin's Primary School, St Martin's

Night

In the sheet of moonlight across the grass,
Trees wail and wave their branches frantically.

The shadow creatures lurk in the shadows,
Waiting for an unsuspecting victim.

The night creatures creep quietly around the garden,
Thick black darkness overcomes the light swallowing it whole.

Howling screeches, shuddering windows,
Leaves rustling in the cold night air.

Out of the window it looks like shape-shifters,
Witches, evil.
Then silence, as the creatures scheme and then stalk.
Bats hang restlessly in trees unknowing of what's going to happen.

As the night starts to fade the creatures sneak away.
Blades of light start to stab the darkness,
To keep it away until night strikes again!

James Rabey (11)
St Martin's Primary School, St Martin's

The Battlefield

They attacked us quietly in the night
And woke us up with a terrible fright.
Hands on triggers, they fired at will
Their only object was to kill.

We fought back with an SMG
And because of that, they began to flee.
We chased them whilst throwing hand grenades
Trying to stop their deadly raids.

With guns blazing, the bullets flew
I killed some soldiers, who I never knew.
Brave young men died just where they stood
Fighting for what they thought was good.

With the dawning of the new day
My friends and comrades, at peace where they lay.
The battle over, fought and won
Each man dead was a mother's son.

Thomas McConnell (11)
St Martin's Primary School, St Martin's

Sunset

A golden sphere hangs in the sky
Gently sinking down, down, down
Brightness disappearing
The moon reappearing
And the sky just turning
To pink, red and gold

The clouds now are woven in the sky
Slowly streaming along, along, along
White and fluffy, so pure
The stars are shining once more
And the sky just turning
To blue, black and grey

Millions of stars hang in the sky
Brightly twinkling silver, silver, silver
Dotted way up high
Where the owls nightly fly
And a canopy now
Hangs over the world.

Stephanie Johns (11)
St Martin's Primary School, St Martin's

The Penalty Shootout

I watch motionless as you put down the ball,
The crowd look on as silent as a mouse,
You turn around and walk slowly back,
Then spin around and run towards me,
As quick as an arrow,
As speedy as a cheetah
And blast the ball,
The crowd's eyes follow the ball towards the goal,
Where I stand on my line,
I dive quickly to my right,
My fingertips reach out and touch the ball,
I catch it in my hands and hold it tightly to my chest.
My team come running towards me,
My heart pounds like a drum,
We cheer and clap our hands,
We have *won!*

Alex Domaille (10)
St Martin's Primary School, St Martin's

Daleks

A shriek of fear, a call of war,
A sudden blast, a fall to the floor.

Skin of metal, not yet found,
A creature of slime, caught, inbound.

'Exterminate' is their favourite word,
They would even shoot a bird.

Sons of Skaro, all hail the Emperor,
Destroying worlds is their doing, or,

Thinking of plans, making ideas,
Some stay separate from their peers.

No one to fear, except . . . for him,
Travelling in his time machine, going to places on a whim.

They've been enemies since time began,
To kill The Doctor, that's the plan.

Troy Le Page (10)
St Martin's Primary School, St Martin's

The Sea
(Inspired by 'Sea Fever' by John Masefield)

I must go down to the harbour again,
where the lonely boat calls for me.
And all I ask is a sunny day,
with a shiny, sparkling sea.
My boat must be strong, fit for storms,
when the evil thunder roars.
And the mad stormy sea is so scarily rough
it could grab with its wet, shining claws.

I must go down to the harbour again,
where the ropes wait to be tied.
My shipmates will be glad to see me
and give a massive cry.
As I look up I see white gulls,
the cheeky birds pecking the ropes.
I know they made a few big holes,
as we set sail I have great hopes.

Joe Weaver (9)
St Mary's CE Primary School, Penzance

The Sea

(Inspired by 'Sea Fever' by John Masefield)

I must go down to the seas again
To find the lonely stairs.
I squat to look at the low piercing sea
And find the bewildered air.
I run to the smear of the crashing wave
And the air-filled sky that rushes.
I get to my feet and stumble to the rocks,
I see the water that crushes.

I must go down to the seas again
to the beaming sea and sky.
And all I ask is a little boat to aim
And a fear to steer it by.
The boat shakes as the rudder shivers
With a fisherman's call in the air.
The lonely men cry with sadness
At the end of their long dare.

Keziah Sutherns (9)
St Mary's CE Primary School, Penzance

Untitled

(Inspired by 'Sea Fever' by John Masefield)

Let's race down to the beach again
To the empty sea and sky
And all I ask is a ship as she sails
And a light to steer her by.
And the wind's whistling a sad song
Bailing out as the boat goes
The crashing waves on the sea's face
As the boat gently flows.

Let's race down to the beach again
For the lonely water's cry.
And all I ask is some good weather
And some blue sky to enjoy.
I'll settle down on board, a break from school
And see the birds flying.
When the tide's going in I'll relax all day
And watch the birds flying.

Kieran Lunn (9)
St Mary's CE Primary School, Penzance

Sea Fever

(Inspired by 'Sea Fever' by John Masefield)

I must go down to the sea again
To the lonely shore of Penzance
And all I ask is a great boat
To steer me off to France,
So I can see the Eiffel Tower
And the green trees blow
And a foggy mist covers the sand
I can just about see it flow.

I must go down to the sea again
And bring a picnic to eat
So I can have a sunbathe
And feel a crab pinch my feet.
And all I ask is a sunny day
So I can have an ice cream.
This day I should remember
Because it was in my dreams.

Katie Lawrence (9)
St Mary's CE Primary School, Penzance

Untitled

I must go down to the sea again
To the crashing waves and the wild sky
And all I ask is a quiet yacht
And a light to steer it by.
And the wind's blow and the wave's splash
And the sails whistle and shake.
As the grumpy mist says goodbye
And I prepare the bait.

I must go down to the sea again
I must see the light blue sky.
It's a blue sky and a cool sky
Which I wish was there all the time.
And all I ask is a wild day
That I wish would always last.
All I ask is to see St Michael's Mount
And the harbour front with the wave's crash.

Paige Maguire (9)
St Mary's CE Primary School, Penzance

The Beach
(Inspired by 'Sea Fever' by John Masefield)

I will go down to visit the sea
To the stormy sea and sky.
And the waves crash into the rocks
As I hear the seals' cry.
Boats in the harbour rock side to side
As the fierce sea cracks the shells
And people's footprints are rubbed away by the tide
And I walk to the sound of the bells.

I will go down to visit the sea
For the call of the flying gulls
And all I ask is a merry boat
That the tide is ready to pull.
A merry sailor at the ready
With the sun reflecting on the sea,
I flee to new and exciting places
To which the wind is ready to pull me.

Elijah Callon (10)
St Mary's CE Primary School, Penzance

Football

Playing football on the field,
Kicked into the goal,
Squealing as I am kicked,
Crying out in pain.

The other balls laughing in laughter,
I am injured today,
Crying ouch in my little eyes
I am stuck in the net, not very happy.
I am being kicked into the mud,
Cross at being dirty.

No one will play with me,
Yeah, I will not get hurt again.

Now I am sad again,
Being hurt now,
Crying out my little eyes.

Chris Barrett (10)
St Neot Community Primary School, Cornwall

Children On The Playground

10.30 is our time
To go to break time in a line.
We go out for half an hour of the day,
While we're out there we have a laugh and play.

It's just like looking at Alton Towers,
My friend has got super powers.
The bigger children mess around,
Hoping they won't get found.
They do get found,
So they decide to have a run around.

Scott Worthing (11)
St Neot Community Primary School, Cornwall

Books

Brand new books
You'll learn to read,
Something new
Will end in mystery.

Adventure, surprise, fiction too,
Lots of fun for me and you.
Poems, plays, information that's new,
Animals set in the zoo.

Everyone take a book,
Keep your head down,
Take a look,
We've got some brand new books.

Harry Potter and Artemis Fowl,
My favourite books,
So now close the book
And put it down.

Daniel Gerry (11)
St Neot Community Primary School, Cornwall

The Office

The secretary just sits there
About to pull out her hair,
The phone suddenly rings,
She's so excited, she sings.
She picks up and says, 'Hello,
Who is it? Could we possibly know?'
They offer a deal on half-price phones,
She slams it down, sits down and moans.
She drinks a sip of tea,
She says hello and smiles at me.
Someone comes in, she thinks *hooray*.
It's only a boy come to pay.
It's boring sitting at the PC,
Just sitting drinking tea.

Jacca Cock (11)
St Neot Community Primary School, Cornwall

The New Playground

The playground's
Watching the children play,
Laughing at their joy,
Dressed in painted markings.

The playground's
Watching the children play,
Wanting to play 'It',
Jealous of being stuck in the mud.

The playground's
Watching the children play,
Caring when they cry,
Crying when they fall.

The playground's
Watching the children play,
The bell is about to ring.
The playground says goodbye.

Barney Wood (9)
St Neot Community Primary School, Cornwall

Playground

We play on the playground,
Every girl and every boy.
Now let's go on the heart line,
Everyone jumping with joy.

When the rain falls down on me,
I feel very upset,
Then the sun comes out
And I feel well again.

All the other playgrounds
Make fun of me,
But I have inspiration
And that's what makes me me.

Tia Wilton (10)
St Neot Community Primary School, Cornwall

The Computer

The computer stared all so mean,
Viruses and learning
And very much clean.

I stare out of the window,
Dreaming with fantasy,
I wonder why my computer's never slow.

The shiny circles go in the slot,
It's not a floppy disk,
The computer's loading on the trot.

Millions of pixels,
So many programmes.
And so beats writing with the pencils.

One hundred more pictures than you can think of,
One thousand more videos than you have seen,
One million more sites than you have ever heard of.

Ross Bellringer (10)
St Neot Community Primary School, Cornwall

The School Office

At day the computer's roaring through the Internet,
At night the computer slows down, waiting for a new day.
When the light goes on I wake up, waiting to be turned on,
My brain ticks away as I wait for a new day.

Ladies work their fingernails to the bone,
Tapping the keyboard all day through,
Drinking their hot tea and coffee
With their biscuits, munching away.

The seats they sit on are soft and fun
With their wheels on their chairs,
Racing across the carpet
And their hydraulic springs going up and down.

Ben Symons (11)
St Neot Community Primary School, Cornwall

Playground

Playgrounds are fun,
Everybody run.
Children screaming with joy,
Every girl and every boy.
Playing with the netball
As they scream and try to run,
Shoot the netball through the big hoop.

There are markings on the ground,
Happy and wild while we're around.
Snakes are some of the markings,
Slithering around but not making a sound.

The playground brings joy
To every child running wild,
But you must be careful, there are rules.

Everybody come and play,
Please don't worry,
You don't have to pay,
Come on everybody,
Come on and play.

Kelsie Worth (10)
St Neot Community Primary School, Cornwall

In The Office

As I watch children go past,
Adults on the computers all day,
Watching the staff type the newsletters.
As the light goes off,
I'm like a lonely cloud in the sky.
I'm on the floor trying to go to sleep,
Dreaming about next week.
Now it's here, the week begins,
Everybody going in and out,
Children coming in, and with their dinner money,
All you hear is *tap, tap, tap* on the keyboard.

Rhiannon Sanders (11)
St Neot Community Primary School, Cornwall

What Am I?

I'm round, I'm soft, but sometimes hard,
I'm enjoyed by most,
Disliked by others.
I'm good friends with a boot,
Same with gloves.
I'm used to flying,
I'm used in attack and defence.

I'll travel anywhere,
I fly through the air like the wind.
I'm played on a pitch,
I'm used in a game,
I'm an amazing piece of equipment,
I get hurt most of the time.

I go head to head,
I'm on the pitch,
But on the sideline,
I'm rolled around,
I make a sound
When I'm kicked around.

What am I?

Adam Gregory (11)
St Neot Community Primary School, Cornwall

Playgrounds And Playing Field

P laygrounds are fun, they are noisy
L azing around on the field
A person has hurt himself, oh dear!
Y eah, having fun!
G rey tarmac, ow, get off me!
R ocky, rough ground, hurts if you fall
O h my, there's Tia, c'mon, let's play!
U h-oh, here comes Mrs Rowe, hide!
N oisy children get sent inside
D one, yay, the day is done!

P laying fields rock, rolling in the grass
L aying around sleepily, Tia's playing brass
A ny time, any place, Mrs Rowe's always there!
Y es, playtime's over, lessons start again
I n time for lessons, hip hip hooray!
N o time to waste, get a pen!
G one to Mr Collins for great work, playtime again!

F un, fun, fun, doing it again. C'mon Tia, play!
I n the sun, too hot, there's a ball!
E verywhere hedges and fields.
L azing around on the field.
D inosaur toys from the boys all over the grass, playtime over.

Amber Johnson (9)
St Neot Community Primary School, Cornwall

Our School

Our school wakes with the birds,
Our school sings with us in assembly,
Our school cries when someone is hurt,
Our school screams when we do PE.

Our school talks to us,
In numeracy, literacy and science.
Our school smiles when she receives a gift,
She is only three years old.

Our school is friends with everyone,
Our school loves to learn,
Our school has a heart,
Our school is a person.

Our school sheds a tear
When we have to leave.
Our school loves us.
I love our school!

Asha Wilton (11)
St Neot Community Primary School, Cornwall

The Field

On a sunny day, the wind
Blows through the dancing grass,
The dew gets burnt up by the sun,
The happy children trample
All the shiny white daisies.

Balls are airborne and whizzing
Fast through the air,
The birds are picking up their tasty seeds.
Long after the bell will ring
And the field will be left in peace.

Liam Parnell (11)
St Neot Community Primary School, Cornwall

Most Computers Come With . . .

As I typed, the keyboard screamed.
A computer is slow or fast.
Now computers come with thin screens
And some are frustration free,
But if not, they will crash.

Some computers come with big hard drives,
While others come with small hard drives.
But some are built for certain things,
Like gaming or work.
No wonder they are slow.

Most computers come with Windows XP or Vista,
Otherwise they are old.
Broadband is very fast,
Much faster than dial-up.
The Internet is very fun,
Games, video and music.

Ben Froggatt (10)
St Neot Community Primary School, Cornwall

Go Rugby

Rugby ball!

The rugby ball screamed,
The foot came to kick it.
Towards the post it soared,
For then the conversion was scored.

Rugby posts!

The rugby posts yelled
As if they'd snapped,
Because of the awesome power
Of the rugby ball.

Ashley Nicholls (11)
St Neot Community Primary School, Cornwall

The Storeroom

Inside the storeroom we have . . .
Special footballs
By the walls,
Round hula hoops
Without the loops,
Gymnastic mats
On top of the racks.

You'll need to use your bones
To jump over these cones.
Tennis rackets
Held up with brackets,
Hockey sticks,
Take your pick.

We have the most
Football posts,
Tag rugby tags
In special bags.
So here we go,
Let's play polo!

Rowen Cunningham (11)
St Neot Community Primary School, Cornwall

Birds

Birds are funny little things,
Some birds fly while they eat their dins.
All birds have beaks
As they carefully seek,
They eat worms and slugs and snails,
But they don't have water pails.
Pigeons, parrots, kingfishers, seagulls,
They're all birds.

Tania Douglas (9)
Sandford School, Sandford

Rhyming Couplets

I want to be a teacher,
I want to say, 'I'll eat ya.'
I want to rule the school,
I want the school to have a pool.
I want the children to behave,
I want to bury them in a grave.
I want to be a teacher,
I want to meet ya.
I want the children to serve me,
I want them to bring me tea.
I want to give them tricky work,
I want to eat chocolates and smirk.
I want to beat ya,
I want to be a teacher.

Lucy Douglas (9)
Sandford School, Sandford

The Thing In The Gutter

It is the end of a school day
And down the bumpy drive
Come laughing, chattering, coat-swiping children.
Annoyed, a tree covers up its ears.
The wind stops still in surprise!

A boy shouts, 'Hey, stop!'
Everybody falls over, looks -
There in the gutter is a baby . . .
Platypus with water-blue eyes and mud-brown fur,
Like a giant peanut of misunderstanding.

Cautiously, *sooo* cautiously,
The boy who had shouted picks him up
And takes him to the safety
Of a nearby pet shop.

An afternoon to remember
On this leafy day in October.

Thomas Edwards (8)
Shirley Junior School, Shirley

At The End Of The School Day

It was the end of the school day,
Out came the children shouting,
With bags swinging,
Racing to the park.
The sun screeched at them
Because of all the noise.

Suddenly they stopped dead,
They looked and stared.
There was something on the ground.
They thought it was an old rag, very frayed,
Just laying on the ground.

They got closer and realised it was a fox.
The fox had the fear of fire flickering in its eyes,
It was all orange with one white stripe across its body.

The oldest girl put her bag down,
Stepped forward, further forward
Until she was an inch away,
Glanced behind her, everybody else staring at her.

She looked forward again, took a deep breath
And carried the creature to the safety of an old oak tree.
They all held their breath, a day to remember,
That warm afternoon in September . . .

Molly Oldridge (8)
Shirley Junior School, Shirley

At The End Of A School Day

At the end of a school day,
The footpath is crowded with arguing,
Shouting, tripping children.

The sky shrinks back in surprise,
The sun moans in pain,
For the noise is deafening.
But the sun still shines
Like a radiator on full blast.

A girl spots something that looks
Like a small ginger fuzzball.
The group skid to a stop,
For the fuzzball is a petrified kitten.
The children stand and stare, eyes bulging.
The girl tiptoes forward, ever so carefully
Scoops up the kitten and places it in her bag.

A boy stares and says to the girl,
'You would take it, wouldn't you?'
And just when the sky and sun think
The noisy parade is over, it starts again.

The shouting, arguing, tripping children
Race along the footpath, the girl trailing behind.
What a lovely day to remember
On this warm afternoon in July.

Olivia Beatson (8)
Shirley Junior School, Shirley

At The End Of The School Day

It's the end of the school day,
Up the short lane come whizzing, shouting children.
The stones jump up in surprise as the children sprint past.
A blue car races them with lots of joy.

Suddenly the children halt,
See a fluffy cushion lying on the black, dusty road,
Stare in surprise as the little thing wriggles
Slightly on the stones.

Small boy thinks for a moment,
Lays his bag on the floor,
Walks over cautiously and picks up the creature,
Puts it under a reaching tree.

The stones settle down and watch with the calm children,
Then the object scampers up the tree.

Nicolas Neves (8)
Shirley Junior School, Shirley

At The End Of A School Day

At the end of the school day,
Coming down the lane came
Bag-dropping, screaming children.
The sun stared down in amazement.

Suddenly the children stopped,
Stared in amazement at a
Hamster like an old spotty orange.

A boy dropped his bag,
Tiptoed over and gently, so gently,
Carried it to the shade of a tree.

Boy, children and sun waited and did
A sigh of relief for the hamster.

Albany Rowan (8)
Shirley Junior School, Shirley

At The End Of A School Day

It is the end of a school day
And through the damp sunny park
Come three children giggling while walking on
The wind wraps its cold blanket around them

They stop suddenly
Stare and gasp
At the little fairy in a glass bottle
She is using all her strength thumping against the glass
Her dress is trembling in a bush
She is like a rainbow shining with a promise

A girl tiptoes forward
And so gently scoops it up
All the others stare in excitement at it

The girl carries it gently to the safety of a bench
Tiptoes away and everyone holds their breath
There is a stunning silence
She suddenly breaks out and everyone cheers.

Imogen Lee (8)
Shirley Junior School, Shirley

At The End Of A School Day

It is the end of a school day
and down the sandy beach
come two children, walking down the crunching sandy beach.
The sun and clouds shout in amazement.

Suddenly the children stop,
frozen to the ground, mouths wide open in surprise,
as they stare at a golden starfish,
laid flat on the sand, like a golden pencil tin.

A girl bends down slowly and picks it up
and carefully she holds it,
then she starts walking toward the ocean,
leaving the others gaping in surprise at the edge of the ocean.

Emily Yeates (7)
Shirley Junior School, Shirley

At The End Of A School Day

It's the end of a school day
and down the road come three chatting children.
The trees whisper to the sky.
The sky gapes in surprise.

The children stop chatting, look straight ahead.
Eyes fill with tears and they gasp
at a big tortoise, curled up in its shell,
like a green and grey football.

A boy drops his bag
and scoops the tortoise up.
Quietly he carries the creature
to the shade of a big log.

Children, boys, trees and sky
hold their breath.
A day to remember
on this warm summer's day in June.

Tom Harman (8)
Shirley Junior School, Shirley

The Miniature Flower

It is the end of a school day,
Five children come down the road
Singing the song that they learnt in music.
They sing so loudly that the flower shouts at them.

Then they gasp.
They see a miniature flower,
It hardly reaches four centimetres.
One of them touches the miniature flower.

The miniature flower jumps,
Then another child steps forward.
They pick it up
And move it to a safe place
Under the shade of an apple tree.

Toby Wilkins (8)
Shirley Junior School, Shirley

At The End Of A School Day

At the end of a long school day
a gang of boys and girls all different sizes
were walking back from school shouting.

The silver moon put two stars in his ears.
He could not hear anything for the noise was so loud.

The gang of children slowed to a stop
but one girl thought she had seen something
in the silvery shadows under the tree.

In the light it shone brightly like a fiery star.
The girl could not believe it,
the moon gaped in surprise . . .

It was a diamond.
The girl picked it up,
still wondering if it was real or not.

The huge diamond shimmered in the moonlight.
The girl put it in her pocket,
something to remember on this warm afternoon in June.

Lydia Keeffe (8)
Shirley Junior School, Shirley

The Baby Dinosaur

At the end of a school day
ten children are streaming
through the gate eating sweets,
the dust on the floor screams.

One backs away,
knocking the rest over,
they all scream at a baby dinosaur
curled up shivering like a lump of jelly.

A girl tiptoes forward,
picks up the creature
and slips it in her pocket quite shyly.

Anna Pugh (8)
Shirley Junior School, Shirley

It's The End Of A School Day

It's the end of a school day
and through the quiet churchyard
come four children blowing gigantic bubbles
down the stony path while the sun shines like a pound coin.

Then suddenly they stop and stare
and their eyes grow bigger than their stomachs.
Lying under a big oak tree a tiny puppy crying for attention
like a golden pillow.

The four girls dump their bags and tiptoe closer.
One of the girls scoops the puppy up
and gives it lots of love and very gently she places the puppy
into her school bag with his head peeping out.
The girls tiptoe home and one of the girls
finds the puppy a lovely bed and some lovely toys.

Joanna Loizou (8)
Shirley Junior School, Shirley

Small And Interesting

It is the end of a school day
and through a stunning rainbow
come two sweet little children
and a gang of boys, coatless.
The rainbow shudders.

Suddenly they stop still,
hold their breath at a small creature
as round as a flower middle,
sat cosily on the soil
as if it was a woolly armchair.
It looks like a golden leaf
coldly sitting down.

A rough-looking boy
gives it to a small-looking girl.
She slowly carries it indoors
to a cosy house on Darning Street!

Rosy-May Schofield
Shirley Junior School, Shirley

At The End Of A School Day

At the end of a school day
three children were walking home.
They were just about to cross the road
when they saw a book.
They grabbed it.
It opened.
The children read.
'This is the magical book of spells,'
they said to themselves.
'Abracadabra turn Mum to a kangaroo!'
Their mums were kangaroos!
They went to their rooms.
They turned their mums back.
They took photos of their mums.
Stuck them in their rooms.
What an exciting moment to remember
on a warm afternoon in June.

Matthew Loizou (8)
Shirley Junior School, Shirley

A Little Ball Of Fluff

It's the end of a school day
And through the quiet field
Come skipping happy children wading through the grass.
The trees are whispering excitedly.

Suddenly they stop and glare,
They gasp excitedly
At a tiny chick
Squeaking with fear.
It looks as soft as a ball of fluff.

A girl dumps her bag and as softly as she can,
Picks up the chick
And takes it to the safety of the bush.
Everybody holds their breath waiting for it to move.

Elizabeth Laybourne (8)
Shirley Junior School, Shirley

The Tale Of A Baby Mermaid

It is the end of a school day
and through the shady trees
come a group of children with a basket of food.
The pondweed sniffs the lovely smell.

Everything stops and stares,
a glimmer of light then a tiny squeal splits the air.
Suddenly they see it's a mermaid, a baby one,
laid down on the ground like a frozen raindrop.

A girl gets the basket,
fills it with water,
then slowly puts her in it.
Excited, the rest gather around her.

Everything, everyone holds their breath,
a moment to remember on this warm afternoon in June.

Katie Rose Sherliker (8)
Shirley Junior School, Shirley

At The End Of A School Day

It is the end of a school day,
Children come rushing to get to the park
As the sun pretends to be in shock.

Suddenly they freeze and gaze,
They see a little bunny
Which looks like a mouldy toy.

A senior boy dumps his bag
And gingerly, so gingerly
Carries the bunny to the safety of an old oak tree.

Boy, children and sun gape,
A moment to remember
On this warm afternoon in June.

Grace Masih (7)
Shirley Junior School, Shirley

At The End Of A School Day

It is the end of a school day
And down the quiet road
Come stone-kicking giggling children,
The road jumps in surprise.

Suddenly they freeze while kicking a stone,
They gaze, still frozen
At a tiny blue tit,
Wings drooped in the middle of the road
Like a piece of fallen sky.

A girl tiptoes forward very quietly,
Scoops up the ball of feathers
And places it in the nearest tree.
Children and road hold their breath,
There is silence in the air,
Then the flapping of wings.

Alice Wheatley (8)
Shirley Junior School, Shirley

On The Church Wall

It is the end of a school day,
through the stony churchyard
come two giggling and laughing children,
the stones jump up and down to them.

One little boy stops, everyone else,
the children stare and get closer
to what looks like an orange ball, but
it is a curled up kitten on top
of a crumbled wall in the churchyard.

A boy chucks his bag
and carefully picks up the creature,
brings it closer and closer,
taking it home holding their breath.

Chloe McArthur (8)
Shirley Junior School, Shirley

The End Of A School Day

It is the end of a school day.
Three children come running down the pavement playing football.
The clouds, the trees and the sun cheer.

The ball rolls into the road.
As quick as a rocket one of them rushes across
and they freeze in amazement,
stare at a dead dragon in the shadow of a car like a bush of thorns.

All three boys try to move the dragon,
tensing their muscles and bending their knees,
faces clenched up with the weight,
but it is too heavy.

Suddenly the dragon absorbs all the sun's energy
and comes back to life.
It flies away roaring out fire.
What a summer's day to remember.

Reuben Benton (7)
Shirley Junior School, Shirley

At The End Of A School Day

It is the end of a school day
and through the grassy field
a couple of children chatting
trees whispering to each other

They slowly stop
take one step back, gasp
at a lonely dragon
tears flowing down its face
twinkling like a pile of rubies

A boy gently strokes it
takes one step back
silently not breathing
a day, a moment to remember
on a spring day in May.

Louis Machin (8)
Shirley Junior School, Shirley

What Happened At The End Of A School Day

It is the end of a school day
And lots of happy children come shouting and playing down
                                        the deserted high street.
The sky becomes deaf because of the noise.
The leaves twirl around them trapping them inside the whirlwind.

But then a baby wolf begins to howl,
It has lost its mum and dad.
It's poor and defenceless.
A girl picks it up carefully, the wind blows her long hair.

It's very weak and untidy, it looks like a snowy table.
She comes and stops everyone, everyone freezes.
She goes, puts it in a bush and gets a pound of meat.
It eats the meat.

Girl, children, sky and sun rejoice
As the baby wolf runs about.
Eventually it steps into the bushes and wishes for its mother.
This happened in 1872.

Phoebe Haste (7)
Shirley Junior School, Shirley

It's The End Of A School Day

It is the end of a school day
and down the alleyway
come three children shouting, gossiping,
wind breathing cool breath.

Children jump to a halt, stare and laugh
at the miniature elephant,
ears shaking under calm breath,
like a ball of grey glitter.

A girl chucks her bag,
scaredly pushes the miniature elephant into her hands,
the girl gently moves,
placing the miniature elephant in a cradle of her jumper, in relief.

Lauren Mara Rickard Foxley (7)
Shirley Junior School, Shirley

At The End Of A School Day

At the end of a school day,
down the road in the noisy park,
two girls sat in a leafy tree,
the wind dancing over to hear them.

They stop and listen,
their eyes widen and tip their heads to one side,
rub their eyes and see a Labrador puppy in a bush
with its tail over its eyes
like a block of gold.

One of the girls picks up the puppy
and put it in her arms softly,
the other girl stares at the puppy.

Charlotte Franklin (8)
Shirley Junior School, Shirley

At The End Of A School Day

It is the end of a school day
and through the leafy common
come two walking and chatting children
the trees whisper to each other
and the ground looks up at the sky

The children stop immediately
eyes widen and slowly they come closer
and stop and stare at an electric sword
on the grassy ground like a yellow fish with a black tail

One of the children picks up the electric sword
speechless puts it in his trousers
and takes it home.

James Matthew Quinn (8)
Shirley Junior School, Shirley

The End Of The School Day

It is the end of the school day,
down the drive came shouting children,
suddenly they came to a silence,
the children were silent,
they stood still.

It was a deserted street,
the children loved the street because it was so quiet,
suddenly they skidded to a stop.
One of them stepped closer
and picked up the very cute hamster.

She took it inside,
smuggled a box with holes into her bedroom,
put the hamster in a box,
called it Cookie.

The children rushed downstairs
to get some nuts for Cookie.
Cookie seemed to like the children.

By the way Cookie is as blond as a newborn giraffe!

Anna Hotston (8)
Shirley Junior School, Shirley

Cockroach

Scuttling in numbers bitterly
Attacking a wooden house
The small cunning little things
Start bombarding a barrier
To dominate another hive
And the vile protector
If you disturb the leader
They may turn on you
The oily shell lets them
Escape *death*.

Nicholas Walker (9)
The Tynings CP School, Staple Hill

The Funny Animals

Here's a poem you should hear
About a dog who loved his beer
He used to drink three pints a day
But now he puts five pints away.

My neighbour's cat had lovely fur
If you met him he would purr
He always snored when he was asleep
And hated food, which was cheap.

My friend's snake has skin like silk
And always drinks a lot of milk
He used to tie himself in a knot
He really is a stupid clot.

I have a beautiful coloured parrot
He sits in his cage and eats carrots
He often likes to sing along
To one of my favourite nursery songs.

Ocean Bracey (10)
The Tynings CP School, Staple Hill

Monster Beings

Now here is a poem that'll get you going,
With its monsterly flowing,
And for everything you know,
There's creatures down below,
Like the dragons that can fly with their powerful wings
And the little fairy that quietly sings
And the unicorns that come out at night
And all of them see the wonderful sight
And when we peacefully sleep at night,
The monsters come out with a nervous fright,
It's safe at night not out late,
Why it's safe because the monsters already ate.

Sasha Morch-Monsted (10)
The Tynings CP School, Staple Hill

Animals In The Forest

Say his name and you will play the game

He sits alone so quiet at night, his hoot may give you a terrible fright
Can you guess? Can you guess?
Say his name and you will play the game

His face looks very sly as he hurries by
Can you guess? Can you guess?
Say his name and you will play the game

He makes his house underground and he is never to be found
Can you guess? Can you guess?
Say his name and you will play the game

They bury their nuts for the cold winter day
When the snow gets so deep they can never play
Can you guess? Can you guess?
Say his name and you will play the game

They gallop, they canter, they run right beneath the sun
Can you guess?

Can you guess?

Vicky Vallis (10)
The Tynings CP School, Staple Hill

In My Imagination

In my imagination
I am a car made of water
Floating over the stars
Shouting out the secrets of the world.
I make planets crumble
And grow like a child
While I go through the door
Of unimaginable dreams.
They beam down like a laser
Connecting the galaxies together
With happiness and peace.

Matthew Blanchard (9)
The Tynings CP School, Staple Hill

What Am I?

I'm quick, I'm fast, I never stop running,
I'm silky soft but big before daring,
I'm brown, yellow as well as spotty,
Looking after my territory,
What am I?

I'm big, I'm tall but weigh a ton,
Squirting, splashing, having fun,
Lazing, lounging in the sun,
I remember everything I've done,
What am I?

I'm brown, I'm furry, I swing around,
You won't catch me on the ground,
I eat vegetables but bananas are best,
Give me time and I'll pass a test,
What am I?

I'm soft, small with a fluffy tail,
I zip around not like a snail,
I jump through fields, maybe gardens,
Too quick for you no need for pardons,
What am I?

Kyra Hopkins (10)
The Tynings CP School, Staple Hill

Car Journey

Firing up the engine,
Running down the road,
Trees swaying in the breeze,
Revving round the corner,
Filling up with fuel,
Lights like lightning,
Wipers like the wind washing off the water,
I'm at my destination, it's the end of the line for me.

Joseph Wood (10)
The Tynings CP School, Staple Hill

Animals

Animals, animals are so cute,
Dogs and cats do not wear suits.
Animals, animals some can fly,
Underwater creatures cannot cry.
Animals, animals that can swim,
Some of them are very thin.
Animals, animals can be pets,
None of them can play duets.
Animals, animals have food every day,
Some of them were born in May.
Animals, animals also need drink,
Only two animals are pink.
Animals, animals don't wear nappies,
Most of them make people happy.
Animals, animals are living every year,
They do not drink human beer.
Animals, animals are very smooth,
Many of them can run fast and move.

Naomi Hall (10)
The Tynings CP School, Staple Hill

Phoenabird

I'm a giant blazing bird
Of the sun and space itself.
I am death, I am love, I am life.
I'm like the destructive fires of Hell,
But brighter than the heavens above!
With my wings as fast as a flickering candle.
I shall launch myself into the farthest reaches of the galaxy,
Where I will rest for all eternity in a never-ending slumber.

Joshua Hughes (9)
The Tynings CP School, Staple Hill

Gymnastics

Gymnastics is great
I know it's my fate.
I train every day to be the best that I can,
My family is my number one fan.
My favourite is bar, I swing round and round,
I do a pike dismount and land on the ground.
To balance on the beam requires great strength,
If you are going to make it down that great length.
Flick high, flick low,
You don't know how it's going to flow.
Stay calm, stay cool
And you won't be a fool.
Floor is fun, you can bounce, flick and fly,
Do your best, all you can do is try.
Vault says my coach, is the hardest of all,
If you don't do it properly, it's likely you will fall.
Competitions come around once every few weeks,
If I do well I get lots of treats.

Laura Flett (9)
The Tynings CP School, Staple Hill

Galloping Horses

Jumping, bucking
Playing with the other horses
Trotting, playing
Galloping in the big green field
Disturbing other horses!
In two months he's going to Turkey
All bright and not dirty
To try a competition
If he wins it he will
Belong to a famous celebrity.

Mitchell Brosnan (10)
The Tynings CP School, Staple Hill

Nursery Rhyme Mix-Up

You know that Baa Baa Black Sheep
Had a lot of soft black wool,
If Humpty Dumpty borrowed some,
(Enough to break his fall).

Then all the . . . king's horses,
And all the . . . king's men,
Would have no need to put him back together again.

They could have joined that,
Duke of York in his march up the hill,
That duke would have 12,000 men
And even more still!

They might have met young Jack and Jill,
On their climb to the top,
But if Jack fell down and broke his crown,
They might have had to stop.

They would have had to stop,
To help young Jack and Jill,
They might have fetched their pail of water,
To be more helpful still.

Now these are some nurs'ry rhymes,
They are a bit mixed up,
But you choose which ones you read
And you choose when to *stop*.

Dominic Porteous (10)
The Tynings CP School, Staple Hill

The Ball Boy

I am the ball, the best ball of them all
I can bounce high right out of the sky
I can juggle as fast as you wish.
I can even do the twist in the mist
I am the ball boy, I am the ball boy.

Jack Mitchell (10)
The Tynings CP School, Staple Hill

Magic Monkey

Running through the jungle,
A metre in the air.
Gazing at the animals,
Playing with their friends.
I grab a branch,
On a huge green tree.
Swinging through the jungle,
A magical feeling of being free.
The hot sun beating down on me,
Making me sweat.
I jump into a river,
Now I'm soaking wet.
I fly to the top
Of a great green tree.
Magically I am dry,
Dry as can be.
In the distance I can hear,
A call from my mum.
A click of my fingers,
Magically I appear back at home.
'Time for bed,' my mummy said,
'Toilet and teeth.
Of course don't forget,
No jumping on the bed.'

Hayden Watkins (10)
The Tynings CP School, Staple Hill

Scrambling Is Fun!

I like racing fast
So I pull back the gas
I fly up the jump
And come down with a bump
Wow I'm a winner at last.

Elliot Lattuca (9)
The Tynings CP School, Staple Hill

How I Wish That I Could Fly

I sat and watched the clouds go by
And pictures came into my eyes.
Trees and flowers rushing by,
Oh how I wish that I could fly.

It seems that now the clouds are black
And I have forgotten to pack my mac.
Oh how I wish that I could fly
Away from this horrible day.

Now the rain is coming down,
It is really making me frown,
But wait, I can see a sunbeam
Shining, though now flying seems
The thing to do.

Dreams and clouds are the best,
If only I could do the rest
And make my life a special one
And fly away to have some fun.

Abbie White (10)
The Tynings CP School, Staple Hill

My Noisy Brother

My brother's such a noisy boy,
When he eats he slurps.
When he drinks milk he gargles.
After meals he burps.
He cracks his fingers when he's bored.
He whistles when he walks.
He snaps his fingers when he sings.
When he's mad he squawks.
At night he snores so loud it sounds like a riot.
Even when he sleeps,
My noisy brother still isn't quiet!

Brendan Turner (10)
The Tynings CP School, Staple Hill

The War

I'm putting on my armour,
I'm no longer a farmer.
A soldier they have made me,
My wife is having a baby.

We are running into war,
My helmet just dropped to the floor,
My head is now a weak spot,
I hope I don't get shot.

We are fighting for our lives,
For the safety of our kids and wives.
I just defeated a big guy,
By stabbing him in his thigh.

The war has ended,
And we have brilliantly defended.
We have triumphed, we have won,
I'm going home to see my son.

Jacob West (9)
The Tynings CP School, Staple Hill

The Never Before

Angrily barking with lovely eye-catching coloured tails, ears.
Their fresh fur like your dreams of tomorrow.
The bouncy, nipping biter,
The furry, hairy friend,
You will have new colour like no other!

Harry Edwards (10)
The Tynings CP School, Staple Hill

The Tiger

Furry, cute but dangerous.
Vicious and protective of its cubs,
Pouncing on prey,
Biting with its long canines.

Creeping quietly through the long grass,
Ready to pounce at any time,
Play fighting, eating food.

Lying down in the afternoon sun,
Drinking water, resting in the pool.
Running around and having fun.

With his young sitting down
Under the old dead tree,
While Mum and the cubs catch tea.

When they return,
He heads down to the water hole,
To have a swim,
Trying to escape his gruesome kids,
But they can smell better than him.

They soon find him having a nap,
They pounce on him just for a laugh.
They all end up in the bath,
The kids splashing in the pool,
Having one last swim,
Then dragging Mum in.

Chris Lewis (10)
The Tynings CP School, Staple Hill

That's Impossible

I'd like to see cats making mats

> But that's impossible
> That's impossible

I'd like to see crops in shops

> But that's impossible
> That's impossible

I'd like to see the police being geese

> But that's impossible
> That's impossible

I'd like to see rats owning flats

> But that's impossible
> That's impossible

I'd like to see kings having wings

> But that's impossible
> That's impossible

But I think anything is possible!

Abigail Bowden (9)
The Tynings CP School, Staple Hill

The Poem Of My Life

This is a poem to get you going about myself and the world I live in.
The world I live in has happy, sad and tough times.
The sad time are when I felt down and unhappy.
The tough times are when bad things have happened to me.
The happy times are when I feel like I'm on top of the world.
This is the end of this poem and the world I live in.

Daniel Sheppard (10)
The Tynings CP School, Staple Hill

Rabbits Or Hares?

Rabbits, rabbits everywhere
But is it a rabbit or is it a hare?
Is it a cuddly velvety creature
Or is it a large-eared wildlife eater?

Rabbits, rabbits everywhere
But is it a rabbit or is it a hare?
Is it your fluffy pet who needs to visit the vet
Or is it Thumper who the farmer met?

Rabbits, rabbits everywhere
But is it a rabbit or is it a hare?
Is it the scurrying animal with the twitching nose
Or is it the enormous animal that eats the rambling rose?

Rabbits, rabbits everywhere
But is it a rabbit or is it a hare?
So have you decided or can you guess?
Are we talking about the hare called Henry or the rabbit called Bess?

Rabbits, rabbits everywhere
Do you really care?

William Stabb (10)
The Tynings CP School, Staple Hill

Oh Please

Oh please, oh please, oh please Miss Shaile
Oh let me come to school by whale
I'll park him in the swimming pool
I know just there he will keep cool

He'll splish and splash and have some fun
I'll pick him up when school is done.

Rebecca Waters (11)
Trewirgie Junior School, Redruth

Our New Cat, Garfield

Our new cat
is rather fat
and is very cuddly too!

He sleeps all day
wakes up to play
and is very cuddly too!

He lays on my bed
after he's been fed
and is very cuddly too!

Garfield
I love you!

Ellie Coleman
Trewirgie Junior School, Redruth

Sunshine

I love to stay in the sunshine,
The sun that shine so bright,
It makes me smile and play every day,
It makes me say I love you sun
And I love to fly my kite.

Jasmin Hoole-Jackson (8)
Trewirgie Junior School, Redruth

Trewirgie

Trewirgie is a place
That puts a smile on your face
We go there to learn
So when we're older we can earn
I love Trewirgie, it's ace.

Bailey Watling (8)
Trewirgie Junior School, Redruth

About The Sea

I love to see the sea
Rolling onto the sand
The waves whooshing over the rocks
Leaving seaweed behind.

The cold fresh air stinging my skin
Seagulls flying above me
Squealing for food
People swimming and surfing
In the huge waves

I love to see the sea.

Isabelle Vincent (8)
Trewirgie Junior School, Redruth

Harvest Poem

The crops are growing in the fields,
The crops are nearly done,
The corn is being harvest as the sun comes up.

The corn is ready to eat
With which you could make so much to eat.

Harvest is nearly over
And the sun turns into rain.

Gemma George (9)
Trewirgie Junior School, Redruth

Dear Mum

This petal's life is done,
But mine and yours have just begun
And as I grow I hope you'll know
I still love you even though
I'll find it hard to tell you so!

Bethany Zammit (11)
Trewirgie Junior School, Redruth

Trampoline

In the sun,
We'll have some fun,
On the trampoline.

We bounce so high,
We reach the sky,
On the trampoline.

Do a flip,
Then pike and dip,
On the trampoline.

When we jump,
We must not bump,
On the trampoline.

We're hot and pink,
We need a drink,
Get off the trampoline.

Caitlin Roach (8)
Trewirgie Junior School, Redruth

Pretty Little Dancer

I'm a pretty little dancer,
I love what I do,
I love to dance on stage
And maybe a show or two.

I'm a pretty little dancer,
I have a best friend
And she loves dancing too,
She's the one I can depend.

I'm a pretty little dancer,
We fly through the air,
Doing jumps and twirls,
All graceful and fair.

Kelly Russell (9)
Trewirgie Junior School, Redruth

Dark And Light

Sitting in hospital by my grandpa's side,
Quiet and still as he lies,
I'm scared, in fact I'm terrified,
With only my family by my side.

I touched his hand and a shiver went up my spine,
At that moment the times we spent together
Went flying by in the midnight sky.

I suddenly thought of the barbecues,
Oh how fun they were
And when we tiptoed in the wood
To find some bears, *grr* . . .

I can remember the beautiful bonfire we had,
It was all very bright and enthusiastic,
He was always there smiling with a great big grin.

Now I bring this poem to an end,
Not all perfect I'm afraid,
But though he's gone
He'll remain in our hearts forever.

Katie McVey (10)
Trewirgie Junior School, Redruth

Weather Sonnet

Bloweth does thou firling breath,
Sweepth through thou windswept trees,
How does thou grawling hands grasp,
My cloak, is clawethed by gnarling fingers,
Pryeth though gnarling fingers shalt not:
For thy hand shall overcome thou grawling mood.

Across thine country,
Flowing rain crasheth upon thy travelling hat,
Soaketh through thy swirling cloak
And dampen thy heart.

Jesse Roach (10)
Trewirgie Junior School, Redruth

My Dog . . . My Cat . . .

My dog Jack

I have a dog called Jack,
His fur is very black,
He likes me to tickle his back.

Jack is so cute,
He is very small,
He makes me laugh when he throws his ball.

My cat Tigger

My cat is called Tigger,
He is brown and ginger,
He chases mice at night,
Which gives them a fright.

My cat eats fish,
He likes them for his tea,
He licks his lips
And purrs at me.

Chloe Dunstan (8)
Trewirgie Junior School, Redruth

My Pets

Bobby

B obby is my dog
O ne time he went for a swim
B obby brings me my slippers
B obby likes his belly being tickled
Y ou would love Bobby too, like I do.

Samba

S amba is my mummy and daddy's dog
A nd she is a boxer
M ost of the time she plays with Bobby
B ut she gets tired, as she is older than Bobby
A nd I love her as well.

Emily Mae Exelby (8)
Trewirgie Junior School, Redruth

The Playtime Poem

Drring the bell goes,
It's playtime!
The playtime rush is big and busy,
It's playtime!
The football thuds and makes girls screech,
It's playtime!
Girls are playing skipping games and chanting rhymes aloud,
It's playtime!
The boys are playing cricket and hitting the ball quite far,
It's playtime!
Then at last, the whistle makes the end and a big rush again,
Playtime's over.

Oh no lessons,
Playtime's gone.
The playground is very empty and silent.
Playtime's over.
I've had a good playtime. It was *fab*.
Playtime's finished!

Emily Youlton (9)
Trewirgie Junior School, Redruth

Bonfire - Fireworks

Whizzing, whizzing round and round,
Dogs barking at the sound,
Howling screamers,
Heard by lemurs.

The sky filled with light,
Who thought it was just a clear night,
Glitter on the trees, glitter in the sky,
Beautiful fireworks no one can lie.

Whizzing, whizzing round and round,
Dogs barking at the sound,
Howling screamers,
Heard by lemurs.

Claudia Dominguez (10)
Trewirgie Junior School, Redruth

My Magic Rug

Playing on my fluffy rug,
The room begins to shake,
The window flings wide open,
My rug soon awakes.

It takes me through the window,
Over the garden gate,
High above the chimney pots,
Riding with my mate.

Soaring through the fluffy clouds,
The pretty cottages below,
Over green fields full of cows
And farmers on the go.

I love to feel the wind,
Crisp against my face,
Swaying side to side,
As my rug enjoys the chase.

A loud yell from below,
Disturbs my final race,
My rug jolts to a sudden stop,
Mum calls, 'Do you want some cake?'

Kensa Jose (8)
Trewirgie Junior School, Redruth

Scooby-Doo

He is brown and black,
He does not slack,
He is the top of the range,
He is top of the charts,
He will never change,
He's got a big loving heart,

Guess what?
It's Scooby-Dooby-Doo!

Bethany Ann Moyle (11)
Trewirgie Junior School, Redruth

Doctor Who Trading Cards

Skinsuit and TARDIS are both ultra-rares
But it seems that nobody cares.
Diseased Man dare touch his face
Because he will run at you at a steady pace.
Slitheen smells of pickled eggs
Although it can be hung by pegs.
Dalek Sec is the best Dalek ever
But it will not be their god, never.
Martha Jones can kill a Dalek
By only using a strip of garlic.
Sycorax love their flight
But they can only fly at night.
Doctor Who cards are the best
Go and put them to the test.

Daniel Matthews (8)
Trewirgie Junior School, Redruth

My Cat

Black and white
colours of my cat,
soft and cuddly
sitting on my lap.

Cute little running shoes
having so much fun,
running in the garden,
playing in the sun.

Hunting at night,
looking for a mouse,
'Please,' says Mummy,
'not in the house!'

Kayleigh Richards (10)
Trewirgie Junior School, Redruth

My Life So Far

When I was zero,
I was not a hero.

When I was one,
Teeth I had none.

When I was two,
I could chew.

When I was three,
I got stung by a bee.

When I was four,
I had a yellow door.

When I was five,
I felt alive.

When I was six,
I ate too much Weetabix.

When I was seven,
I went to Devon.

When I was eight,
Pie I did hate.

When I was nine,
I learnt not to whine.

Now I'm ten,
I can tell you about Big Ben!

Naomi Rogers (10)
Trewirgie Junior School, Redruth

Boring Teachers

When you get ten out of ten,
The teachers don't say yippee!
Just well done not great.
How boring can they be?

You whisper in class,
Because the teacher starts to dwell.
They simply say, 'Stay in at break!'
Why can't they make lessons go well?

When you are late for lessons,
The toilet's where you've been.
A ticking off is what you get.
Whoever made teachers, why are they really mean?

Shannon Massey (9)
Trewirgie Junior School, Redruth

Dodo

There was a bird that lived,
a long time ago,
it's been 300 years
since he walked along the ground.
He likes to eat fresh fruit,
with his large hooked beak.
He nested on the ground,
as he had a big fat belly
and two stubby wings,
so could not fly around.
He wasn't the most beautiful bird,
but the dodo was the most extraordinary.

Bethany Rutter (8)
Trewirgie Junior School, Redruth

Nature's Beauty

N ature is all around us.
A nimals scamper in the meadows,
T rees shade the woodland glen,
U nder the trees the squirrels hunt for nuts,
R abbits bounce and jump to a springtime song,
E verywhere the winter snow is melting.
S pring lambs bleat a happy tune.

B uttercups glisten in the spring sunshine,
E verywhere you look nature sings life's beat,
A ll around flowers burst open in a rainbow of colours.
U ntil the daytime turns to night,
T hen owls hoot a warning tune,
Y ou will always feel happy when nature sings.

Harry Littlejohns (8)
Trewirgie Junior School, Redruth

The Haunted Horse Of Heritron

If you want to see the haunted horse of Heritron,
you must go down to the old musky Scanton stables,
where it lies on the tall hay beds.

Knock on the tall brown doors,
shout, 'Hell horse hell horse,
do come out oh please, please, please!'

From now on stay way back,
as you may get a very, very nasty surprise!

On the tall hay bed at the very back,
lies the haunted horse of Heritron.

Jacob Woodbridge (8)
Trewirgie Junior School, Redruth

My Cat Called Pixie

Pixie is my cat,
She likes to lay on her mat.
She's a very cheeky cat,
But I don't care about that.

She's got her little paws,
With very sharp claws.
She likes a little tickle
Under her chin
And that's where I always begin.

She thinks it's extremely scrummy,
When I tickle under her tummy
And finally she climbs upon my bed
And lays down her weary head.

Saffron Blake (7)
Trewirgie Junior School, Redruth

Oh Little Ladybird

Oh little ladybird,
Look at all your spots,
You have lots and lots and lots.

Oh little ladybird,
Look at all your spots,
I love you,
Lots and lots and lots.

Oh little ladybird,
Time to say goodbye,
Off you go now,
Flutter, flutter by.

Molly Buckland (8)
Trewirgie Junior School, Redruth

Snowman

With coal-black eyes and carrot nose,
I have no fingers, legs or toes,
My skin is icy cold to touch,
Yet you don't see me wearing much!
A woolly scarf, a battered hat,
I'm lucky if I'm dressed in that!
I can't lift my arms, run round or bend,
But I make a wonderful playtime friend.
I'm only around for awhile each year
And you never know when I'll disappear.

Ashley Sweet (8)
Trewirgie Junior School, Redruth

Minibeasts In The Garden

On a hot sunny day all the minibeasts come out to play,
Buzzy bee under a tree and a mini ant is eating a plant.
The first ever spider to ride a glider,
A slug looking for some grub down at the pub.
The millipede takes the lead, poor snail is at the tail.
A bluebottle fly is a nuisance in the sky
and the hornet is after the cornet!

Fynley Caudery (8)
Trewirgie Junior School, Redruth

Elements

Wind the bringer
Earth the giver
Water the sustainer
Fire the taker
Of life we love.

Connor Wrigley
Windlesham House School, Washington

The Girl

Day by day he gazed upon her,
An angel born to Earth,
A star tossed into the sky,
Yet he did not know her name,

Her scent is of fresh daisies,
Her hair a twist of gold,
Her singing of sweet melody,
Yet he did not know her name.

Time passed and passed,
And he stared and stared,
And one day she looked back
And then everything changed.

This feeling could touch the sky,
This feeling could fill the ocean,
This feeling could put out fire,
Is this love?

Benjamin Grant
Windlesham House School, Washington

Fire

Roaring like a pride of lions
Like a phoenix swirling through the air
A welcoming mass of warmth
Chatting away in the great outdoors
Burning away and frolicking around
Licking at the burned wood
Trying to escape
A powerful presence above all others
Growing evermore
Pieces of wood flickering on and off
A Mexican wave moving up and down
Vivid colours bursting out of the wood
It pops, licks, sparkles and flickers.

James Line (11)
Windlesham House School, Washington

What It Means To Be Free

Freedom,
Bounding into a poppy field,
Lying down gazing at the sky
For hours.

Freedom,
Carelessly running,
Along a sunbathed shore
Moist sand squelching
Through your toes.

Freedom,
To be yourself no matter what,
Not caring whether
You are teased or not.

Freedom,
Feel as free as a bird,
Believe you can soar
At any moment.

Freedom.

Imogen Rough (11)
Windlesham House School, Washington

Fire

Fire, glowing like the sun rising from the sky,
Fire, shadowing all the people around.
Fire, where sparks flicker from where there is no darkness.
Fire, a mesmerising element where chaos erupts.
Fire, towering, overtaking the hopeless wood.
Fire, an enclosed murderer where pain rushes through.
Fire, where everything is rushing away from the raging terror.
Fire, an unwelcoming sign of danger.

William Dawe (11)
Windlesham House School, Washington

Aria

Cavorting amongst the highest of trees,
Tumbling with rain and snow.
Aroma wafts travel with the breeze
And hushed whispers are gently blown.

Tasted, smelt, felt, heard,
Yet you will not allow us to see.
Eclipsed, concealed, hidden, obscured
Under a blanket of invisibility.

So much freedom and no boundaries,
Is there a neck to tie a harness?
Will you stay forever free,
Or carry on this lackadaisical dance?

An escaped breath of stabbing gales
Cries out in lamentable song.
And echoes of stunning miserable wails
Howl all night long.

She carries her waltz through sinister and light
In all land, all sky, everywhere.
She is with us right now and all through her flight
She gushes everywhere for she is air.
She cries, brings, flies, sings, hides everywhere
For she is air.

Katharine Stocker
Windlesham House School, Washington

Untitled

Slowly filling silent sails which are pulling out to sea
Breathing on the backs of sailors
Rising and falling with the birds
Gliding through the tops of trees
Unseen but elemental
Essential for survival
Timeless but eternal
Ever close from the beginning to the end of life.

Sam Fiddian-Green
Windlesham House School, Washington

Fire

Fire,
The glooming of the flickering flame.

Fire,
The lighting of the heavens.

Fire,
The mesmerising cross of light.

Fire,
The world of the glowing orb.

Fire,
The licking and the devouring of the forest.

Fire,
The colours of the world.

Fire,
The chattering of the Devil.

Fire,
The feel of entrapment.

Fire,
The never-ending flickering flame.

Fire,
Is the source of the world.

Oliver Micklewright (11)
Windlesham House School, Washington

Water

We stop . . .
Dare I go out onto the burning sand?
Mum says, 'Go!'
We rush, my feet burning,
Then the burning stops.
A trickle of water touches my toes.
I look down
I made it!

Harry Goodwin (12)
Windlesham House School, Washington

Le Rue C'est Blue

With the sound of a ping
It pops out of the spring
And as the wind blows
It trickles and flows

It rolls over leaves
On its quest to the seas
But most will plummet
From the wet mossy summit

As it descends
Down through the falls
Its joyful descent
Surely enthrals

It hits the bottom
And explodes like cotton
And continues its mission
To the depths of the sea

Playing and slaying
Falling and trawling
Flowing its course
Away from the source

It's a wonderful thing
The path is true
It's a source of power et
Le rue c'est blue.

Fergus Simpson
Windlesham House School, Washington

Water

Still water broken by a stone that
Punches the water's surface,
Ripples encircle the stone as it wobbles its way down
And hits the riverbed,
The sound rises up from the vibration.

Georgina Boden
Windlesham House School, Washington

Air

Air creates peacefulness as it brushes past your ear
making a soft whistle.
It is the soft, gentle, gliding touch of the wind.

Air brings about destruction and chaos.
It is the hurricane that twists and turns in savage rage
destroying everything in her path.
It is the furious sound of clashing winds
and the crashing of thunder.

Air is all powerful.
Like standing on the edge of a cliff feeling the harsh winds
pushing against you.
It is a rush of excitement and the shiver of fear.

Air is emptiness and depression,
as if you are in a world of your own,
floating in a calm, quiet space of imagination.

Chris Dawe
Windlesham House School, Washington

Fire

Trapped flames: trying to escape from their wick,
but they will never be free.
Flickering flames: dancing around the fireplace,
teasing the logs.
Destructive flames: annihilating all their path.
Raging flames: causing chaos and damage
like the stampeding of elephant.
Merciless flames: nothing can stop the mindless fire.
Terrible flames: bringing fear to even the bravest of men.
Destructive flames: burning buildings into rubble
and trees into ash.

Cruel, cruel flames.

Charlie Perry (11)
Windlesham House School, Washington

Elements

And from his hands water flowed,
Which filled the many seas and bruised the skies.
It rushed through the valleys and lapped at the shores,
The trickles and droplets which grew to mighty, gushing rivers
And idyllic lakes which stand clear and still as glass.

And with his fists he struck the ground and fire was unleashed.
A fearsome flame which twists and curls,
With its fiery tongue outstretched it licks and chews and spits,
It jumps and dances in the breeze and flickers in the shadows,
It grows forever stronger, the fearsome demon, unstoppable.

And with just one breath the air gushed
Which shifts the tree and ripples the lush green fields.
So flowed limitless nothingness that is everywhere and everything,
That filled the many lungs. The breath of life.

And with his palms he sculpted the earth,
The ageless supporter of life
Where from plants sprout and grow.
His home for many, the canvass for his vast painting.
The elements created.

Miranda Holliday
Windlesham House School, Washington

Air

She gives out life in a baby's first breath
And snatches it away again in a man's dying words.
She curls and twirls and whispers in your ear,
She hisses through holes and sings through cracks,
And watches slyly in the sky and then
She rips across the land as a terrible scream
And tears away lives in careless wrath.
The world trembles when at last she withdraws,
But she knows all, sees all, with her watchful eye,
The ageless, infinite watcher in the sky.

Alastair Maude
Windlesham House School, Washington

Water

Dripping and oozing as I squeeze over the rocks
Thundering and dancing as I soar over the land
Twisting and turning as I splash and plop
As I enter the river
Jumping and sloshing as I hurry
White horses flee as the rapids approach
Tossing and turning as I am thrown from side to side
With nowhere to go but straight
Frothing and flaring as I begin to slow
Flowing down, down, down I fall
As the white horses jump and flee as we tumble
And turn as we are tossed down the waterfall to
Be joined again
As we rush towards our friend the sea
Up and down the waves take me up and down as
We flow over the horizon.

Claudia Thornett
Windlesham House School, Washington

Air

Air, the breath of freedom, the scent of life,
The singing breeze surrounding all,
The soft melody of endless existence,
The voice of a whispering soul.

Air, the almighty power of destruction,
She howls through streets and cities,
The wanderer of the night,
Yearning to be set free.

Air, she dances the waves with her hands,
As if a puppeteer she sweeps the shore,
Gasping at the ecstasy of flight,
She hushes the dunes with her song.

Grace Lee
Windlesham House School, Washington

Water

Water, *serene*
Slowly, gliding down,
Down the rivers, down the streams, water

Water, *chilly*
Freezing over like a bullet, *shiver*
Cool, as it trickles down,
Down the rivers, down the streams, water

Water, *adorable*
The beauty of the early morning,
Watching the still dew flow off,
Down the rivers, down the streams, water

Water, *lush*
As the morning birds drink
Watching a feather float off,
Down the rivers, down the streams, water

Water, *soothes,*
Healing, treating wounds, sending their ills away,
Down the rivers, down the streams, water.

Lily Hinton
Windlesham House School, Washington

Water

So soothing and peaceful
it gently trickles down the rocks.
As it draws closer to the edge
 it gathers anger then topples onto the seashore
where its white horses charge over the sand.
It rides deeper, deeper giving back to the ocean
and then it celebrates, a feast of giant waves,
crashing thunderously.
With every vibration the waves grow wild,
splashing out their rage then withdrawing once again.

Daniel Poulton (11)
Windlesham House School, Washington

Water Poem

I am around you
Below you
Above you
I am you

I have fish and sharks in my belly
Oil spillages over my toes
I have whales hunting in my mouth
And helpless mortals clinging for life in my grasp

I rule over the world
But twice a day I shrivel away
As if in fear

People use me
People play with me
People fear me
People need me
People crave me
What am I?

I am water.

Adam Miller
Windlesham House School, Washington

Water

I watch the white horses charging inland,
Only to be forced back by the pull of the tide.
I can feel the excitement in the air,
The water gently brushing my skin;
The salt makes it tingle like pins are being poked at my flesh.
I feel the power of the waves as they wash over me.
I hear the menacing cry of the gulls circling above me and the gentle
        rhythm of the waves sweeping the shore clean of lies.
This is a paradise,
A friend to all,
A home to the homeless,
And a happiness for those who are sad.

Millie Sparkes
Windlesham House School, Washington

Water

Water
Freezing, chilly
Shivering in the cold morning

Water
Crushing, splashing
Running in-between the rocky banks

Water
Calmly, serenely
Sleeping in the navy ocean

Water
Flying, gliding
Falling from the blue sky

Water.

Zi Yuan Qu
Windlesham House School, Washington

Water

I rush up the beach
I trickle down mountains
I flow from taps
I'm water

I tickle toddlers' toes
I cradle the boats
I make myself heard
I'm water

People play at my toes
People swim at my legs
People surf on my shoulders

For I am water.

Charlie Fenn
Windlesham House School, Washington

Young Writers Information

We hope you have enjoyed reading this book - and that you will continue to enjoy it in the coming years.

If you like reading and writing poetry drop us a line, or give us a call, and we'll send you a free information pack.

Alternatively if you would like to order further copies of this book or any of our other titles, then please give us a call or log onto our website at
www.youngwriters.co.uk

**Young Writers Information
Remus House
Coltsfoot Drive
Peterborough
PE2 9JX**

(01733) 890066